BOUNCING BACK:

Community, Resilience & Curiosity

Isao Fujimoto

Fujimoto, Isao
   Isao Fujimoto : Bouncing Back: Community, Resilience & Curiosity. Sacramento : I Street Press, 2017

ISBN-10: 1546914250
ISBN-13: 9781546914259

Library of Congress Control Number: 2017940904

This memoir is dedicated to my parents
Ayako & Taichi Fujimoto

And to my children
Caedmon, Basho & Esumi Fujimoto

TABLE OF CONTENTS

Chapter One

Bouncing Back

Nanakorobi Yaoki"

"Fall down seven times, get up on the eighth."

The red papier-mâché doll shown on the cover of this book is called a d*aruma*. It is a common and beloved figure in Japan, found in homes, schools, teashops, and temples. The doll is modeled after Bodhidharma, a Buddhist monk who lived during the fifth or sixth century AD and is considered the founder of Zen Buddhism in China. According to legend, Bodhidharma sat facing a wall in meditation for nine years without moving, causing his legs and arms to fall off.

The *daruma* is a symbol for "bouncing back," or what we might call "resilience." Even when the *daruma* is pushed over, the flat-bottomed doll gets up again, independently and without hesitation. Because of this, there is a saying that accompanies the doll: "*Nanakorobi yaoki.*" which translates to "fall down seven times, get up on the eighth." In other words, never give up. No matter how many times we — or our loved ones, our community — are knocked to the ground, we can get up again. People are encouraged to set a goal and blacken one of the *daruma's* eyes. Once the goal has been reached, the other eye is blackened in gratitude for the *daruma's* spiritual help in accomplishing the goal.

The ability to bounce back from injustice and hardship is the story of my family's life. Time and again we faced unexpected challenges: incarceration during World War II, the threat of deportation afterwards, the death of three siblings, an array of health problems – just to name a few. Yet every time we were able to get back on our feet and carry on. This was possible, in large measure, because we lived in a tightknit, caring community, and because our family and friends were strong and resilient like the *daruma*.

My father's equanimity and trust in this process of "bouncing back" showed whenever a child or grandchild came to him whether in tears or happily telling him of their success. Like the story of the Chinese farmer whose son was thrown off a horse – much to the villagers' chagrin, until they learned this misfortune had saved the son from being recruited into the army – my father knew that things are always changing. What seemed terrible could later prove to be a blessing just as a bit of good fortune could sometimes turn sour. Learning how to stay in the moment and depend on one's own inner strength, as well as one's family, in times of hardship and success alike was a gift imparted to me by my parents. So, too, was their willingness to work hard, help their community, and stand up for justice.

As I complete this memoir, it is the spring of 2017. This is a difficult time for many in the United States and throughout the world. Hate, discrimination, and violence appear daily on the front pages of our newspapers and in the constant news feeds of social media. There have been calls to build a wall to keep immigrants from Mexico and Central America from entering the United States. Police shootings of persons of color are a frequent occurrence in cities and small towns across America.

Terrorist attacks at home and abroad have left many fearful. The President has responded by repeatedly issuing a travel ban on Muslim-majority nations, a ban that so far has been ruled unconstitutional. Others have advocated that Muslim Americans should be registered and put in internment camps, as Japanese Americans were in WWII. According to the Southern Poverty Law Center, hate crimes have increased dramatically since the 2016 Presidential election. There are reports of white men pulling hijabs off of Muslim American women, children bullying their Hispanic classmates, and Ku Klux Klan members and Neo-Nazis openly celebrating the election of a man who has shown himself to be a bigot.

Sadly, the tenor of these times is all too familiar to me. My hope is that the story of my life and family will encourage others to stand up to injustice today, drawing strength from their communities and spiritual traditions, and working together for the common good.

Chapter Two

Father Comes to America

My Father's Birthplace

My father, Taichi Fujimoto, was born in 1906 in the fishing village of *Esumi-mura* in Wakayama Prefecture, located on the southeastern tip of Honshu Island in Japan. *Esumi-mura* means "living on the high waves." The picturesque village backs into a forest of spruce and pine. Between the ocean and the mountains is a strip of land for rice paddies and vegetable gardens. Hordes of monkeys descend from the forest to pilfer whatever is ripening in family plots. The sea has served for centuries as the village's main source of sustenance and livelihood.

In my father's time, the village was home to a sizable number of families. He attended the village elementary school along with several hundred pupils. He and his family joined the community in activities and rituals at the nearby Zen Buddhist temple and Shinto shrine. All three of these institutions still exist today but the village has grown quite small due to emigration. When my daughter Esumi – named for the village - attended her grandfather's school eighty years later in 2003, only thirty-one pupils remained.

As a young man, Taichi worked with the village carpenter and later received further training as an apprentice at the Imperial Palace in Tokyo. Some of the houses he helped build are still occupied in *Esumi-mura* today.   Because of limited economic opportunities in the village, Taichi left Esumi-*mura* to serve as the carpenter on the *Milano*, a ship that hauled lumber between Kobe, Japan and Anacortes, Washington. He left behind his parents (Komakichi and Toyo), his older sister, and two younger brothers.

Getting Off the Milano

On Taichi's third voyage on the *Milano* in 1927, he told the captain that he was going to stay in America. He was 21 years old. The captain gave my father ten dollars and wished him well. Another shipmate, who had been promised a job in New York, also got off. Together they walked eighteen hours from Anacortes to Seattle, a 78-mile journey. They found lodging in a section of the city where Japanese immigrants had congregated. In his room that night, Taichi found a Japanese ethnic newspaper. Such papers were published all along the coast from Los Angeles to Seattle, as they were a major form of communication for Japanese immigrants. One news story caught his eye: it was about a Japanese fishing boat that had been found adrift, its entire crew

6

dead. The boat had been carried by the Black Current, which flowed from Japan to the Aleutians and then southward from Alaska and Canada. The dead fishermen were all from the village of Wabuka, one train station stop away from *Esumi-mura*. The newspaper reported that the Wakayama Prefectural Association in Seattle had recovered the fishermen's bodies and prepared them for shipment back to Wabuka.

Of the 47 prefectures in Japan, those with the largest number of emigrants to America at the turn of the twentieth century were Hiroshima, Yamaguchi, and Wakayama, all located in the Western part of Honshu Island. Another large group of Japanese emigrated from Kumamoto, on Kyushu Island. Japanese from each of these regions formed their own village and prefectural associations in America as a way of providing valuable aid to their members and the communities from which they hailed.

Arriving in Yakima.

It was through the Wakayama Prefectural Association in Seattle that Taichi learned several families from *Esumi-mura* were farming in the Yakima Valley, 180 miles from Seattle in the South-Central part of Washington State. After my father arrived in Wapato, Washington, he made his way to the nearby Yakima Indian reservation where over 100 Japanese immigrant families were farming.

The reason he found so many Japanese immigrants farming on the Yakima reservation was due to the passage of the Alien Land Law following World War I. Earlier Japanese immigrants had gained a well-earned reputation for being successful farmers. In California, they produced 50 to 100% of the many fruits and vegetables growing there. Crops ranged from artichokes, broccoli, and beans, to strawberries and flowers.

Rather than being admired for their hard work, however, Japanese immigrant farmers were met with resentment and retaliation by white farmers. At the time, no immigrant from Asia, with few exceptions, could become a U.S. citizen. This would not change until the passage of the McCarran Act in 1952. The Alien Land Law stated that, "people not qualified for citizenship could not lease or buy land." Passed by seventeen states, the Alien Land Law was implicitly aimed towards Japanese farmers, and attempted to shut down Japanese immigrant farming. California passed its Alien Land Law in 1913, Washington in 1921.

However, Indian reservations – like the Yakima reservation – were under the jurisdiction of the U.S. Department of Interior, which meant that they were not subject to state Alien Land Laws. The Yakima Indians were the only people willing to rent land to Japanese immigrants in the area. As a result, thriving Japanese immigrant communities arose around the towns of Yakima, Wapato, and Toppenish.

So it was here – in Wapato – where my father decided to settle. Taichi worked as a farm hand with the Fukiage family for several years. He married my mother, Ayako Tanaka, in 1932 when she was sixteen years old. It was an arranged marriage.

Unlike my father who was an *Issei,* or first generation Japanese immigrant in America, my mother was known as a *Kibei*, a person born of Japanese immigrant parents in the U.S. but educated in Japan. Her father, Yasumatsu Tanaka, emigrated to America by way of Mexico, walking across the shallow parts of the Rio Grande until he eventually reached Washington State. There he married Okuno Kakimoto. Together they worked in the salmon canneries in Ketchikan, Alaska and in the lumber town of Mukuteo, Washington. My mother was born in Seattle. While her parents worked, Ayako was stashed safely away in open drawers and boxes nearby; she became known as "*hako musume*" or the "little girl in a box."

To spare their children from the harsh living conditions of immigrants in Washington, Yasumatsu and Okuno sent their children to Kushimoto, Wakayama, Japan, a small town near my father's birthplace, to be raised by their Grandmother Kakimoto. Ayako was three years old when she made this journey with her brother, Yuzuru, who was five years old at the time, and her one-year-old sister, Mitsuye.

It would be ten years before the children returned to America. When she returned to Seattle, Ayako attended a school for immigrants while her parents ran the Togo Hotel. But when the Great Depression forced them to shutter the hotel, the family decided to relocate to the Yakima Indian Reservation in Wapato. It was here that my mother met the man who would be her husband for the next 68 years.

As will become apparent, my father's journey to America and his training as a carpenter were to play a major role in my family's life. He took a huge but necessary risk in coming to America, a young man in search of new opportunities. But he did not do this alone. From the beginning, my parents were part of a larger Japanese immigrant community in Wapato – and beyond - that would sustain us all.

Chapter Three

Life in the Yakima Valley

Early Years

I was born in Wapato, Washington on September 28th, 1933, the first of what would be Taichi and Ayako's thirteen children. My name "Isao" means "honor" or "merit," and it reflects the expectations and hopes my parents had for me. Our surname "Fujimoto" meant the "source or base of wisteria." My father is said to have watched carefully as a doctor delivered me at home. Following along with an obstetrics manual, my father made sure the doctor was doing everything right. This experience would come in handy later, when my father delivered several of my other siblings during the years we were in the Yakima Valley.

After my parents' marriage, my father began renting and farming 80 acres of land on his own on the Yakima reservation. The first farm I remember was on Old Wapato Road near the Yakima River. On one occasion, my father took me out to the middle of the river in an abandoned canoe. As I looked into the water, I was amazed to see the river teeming with fish so plentiful they looked like they were rubbing against each other as they swam.

Living on reservation land, I would often see Yakamas walking by our house as they cut across our fields. One evening I had an interesting visitor. I had started collecting pennies and enjoyed dumping out my jar and counting how many I had. As I was engrossed in this activity one night I looked up and saw a Yakama standing at the window watching me. I was five years old at the time and very surprised. Quickly, I slid my hand across the flat surface of the table, pushing all the pennies into my jar. When I told my father of this encounter, he just chuckled. He told me the Indians were friendly and my visitor was probably just intrigued by what I was doing.

A Yakama named Old Tom lived in a small cabin on the plot of land we rented. The older Yakamas still spoke the Yakima language. The Japanese immigrants, unsurprisingly, primarily spoke Japanese. Since neither the elder Yakimas nor the Japanese families on the reservation spoke English, I later asked my mother how she had communicated with Old Tom. "Oh, we used our hands," she replied.

A Shared Language

But there was one language both the Japanese and the Yakima could understand: baseball. The reservation had a team called the Yakima Indians; the immigrants' team was named the Wapato *Nippons*. In addition to playing against each other, both the Japanese and the Yakima communities would come together to watch as barnstorming teams passed through the Yakima Valley. For me, the most memorable team was the House of David. This team raised funds and recruited adherents for the Israelite House of David, a religious colony established in Benton Harbor, Michigan. The team attracted a lot of attention as all the players had long hair and were heavily bearded, a practice of their religious faith. Sometimes during one of their games, the ball would mysteriously disappear. After much searching, the ball would eventually be discovered under the beard of one of the House of David players.

As a boy I thought the Yakima Indians were pretty good players. So when I started playing and learned about the Major Leagues, I became a fan of the Cleveland Indians. At the time, I thought teams were named for who they were and what community they represented. When I discovered there were no Indians on the Cleveland Indians, I dropped them. Later, when I started playing baseball in high school, I rooted for the Yankees like all my teammates. I soon realized the reason for their choice. In the late 1940s the Yankees had players like Phil Rizzuto, Yogi Berra, and Joe

Dimaggio. My teammates went by names like Casalegno, Trifilo, Fantozzi, and Romero. The Yankees got their support because they were actually the New York Italians.

Japanese Immigrant Community

We may have been living in America on an Indian reservation, but our identity as Japanese immigrants remained strong. In the early years a variety of itinerant specialists visited the Japanese immigrant communities on the reservation. These included Judo instructors, Buddhist priests and Japanese food merchants. The latter were sent monthly by the Asia Trading Company in Seattle. Their trucks would visit every Japanese immigrant farmstead throughout the Yakima Valley selling items like *wakame* (dried kelp), *nori* (dried seaweed for sushi wrapping), *miso* (soybean paste), *konyaku* (dried agar) and *yokan* (sweets made from *azuki* beans). These items are familiar today to a broad array of sushi-loving Americans but a century ago they were completely unknown to those outside the ethnic community.

Another practice unique to the immigrant community in which I grew up was the saving of umbilical cords for every newborn. Portions of the dried cords were used to treat stomach ailments. Today the medical basis for such folk medicine has taken on new meaning. Stem cells from umbilical cords, for example, are now thought to potentially treat a variety of illnesses. Another practice I recall was seeing my mother spray my father with salt before he was allowed entry into the house after attending a funeral. Salt is used for purification in Japanese culture. This is the reason it is commonly used at the start of sumo wrestling matches.

Though spread out over the countryside, my family and others came together on numerous occasions. The cluster of Japanese stores adjacent to the Buddhist temple in Wapato provided congenial gathering spaces. Especially popular was the auditorium annex to the temple. My father supervised the construction of the annex, drawing on his training and experience as a carpenter at the Imperial Palace in Tokyo. The auditorium soon became a favorite site for bazaars, festivals, judo and basketball events, and productions by visiting thespians.

One of the events I remember fondly was the showing of silent Japanese movies. "Silent movie" is misleading, however, since projectionists had memorized the entire script and supplied the characters' voices. The projectionist of a silent film is therefore aptly called a *"benshi"* or "film narrator" in Japanese. The integral role and skill of the *benshi* was such that "talkies" took hold in Japan much later than in other countries.

Elementary School

When I began first grade at Wapato Elementary School in 1939, I didn't understand much of what my teacher said since she spoke only in English. But I learned quickly, as much from my classmates as my teacher. My classmates included Yakamas from the reservation, children of Wapato merchants, and friends from the Japanese immigrant families.

As soon as school was over, I walked to the Japanese section of Wapato for Japanese language class like most of my immigrant friends. I discovered there were many differences between English and Japanese. This included how each language expressed the sound of animals. In the stories read to us in first grade in elementary school, dogs went "bow wow." In Japanese school dogs barked "wan, wan." Pigs said "oink, oink" in English but "bu, bu" in Japanese. Other examples were "peep, peep" versus "pio, pio" for chicks, "meow, meow" versus "mew, mew" for cats and "cockle doodle doo" versus "koke kok ko" for roosters. I've since learned that all cultures have their special voices for animals and that it is great fun to share how animals sound with people from around the world.

There were other surprises in store for me as I visited with my friends in their homes. Among the

16

crops we grew in the Yakima Valley were corn and potatoes. When we ate these foods at home, they looked just like they did coming from the field. Corn on the cob was visibly corn, fried or baked potatoes were clearly potatoes. So I was bewildered when I visited a friend and watched his elder brother take out a box from the cupboard and fill a bowl with some flaky materials. He added milk and sugar to this after school snack and ate it with a spoon. I asked my friend Sho what was in the box. He told me it was something called "corn flakes."

Several years later I would have a similar experience when I encountered a bag of thin, flaky items in a bag. The pieces were much larger than corn flakes and were salted. I learned they were called "potato chips." What is familiar to us may take on a completely different character after it is processed through a factory or translated into another language. This is as true for corn and potatoes and the sounds of cats and dogs as it is for people and places.

School Lunches

School lunch in those days cost five cents. But instead of a nickel, I paid for my school lunch with a ticket. My father got a roll of these tickets in exchange for the sacks of potatoes and carrots he contributed regularly to the Wapato school cafeteria.

Others paid for the school lunches with tickets also. One was my classmate Harold. His family had moved to Wapato from a far away place they called the "Dust Bowl." Those who came from this part of the country were called "Okies" in town. I could tell by the clothes Harold was *not* wearing that his family was having a very hard time. He wore beat up shoes but no socks. He wore overalls but very little else. When we went to the school clinic to get a health check up, the attendant wrapped a towel around Harold as he had no underwear.

We all struggled during the Depression. But Japanese immigrant families helped each other. For families like ours, poverty was made bearable by a sense of community. For families like Harold's, the situation was a lot tougher.

The Meaning of Community

The meaning of community was underscored for me one spring on our farm. During the winter months my father and neighboring farmers had been working on the building of the *kaikan*, the auditorium annex to the temple. But once the spring planting season arrived my father's work force disappeared. My father, however, was determined to finish the auditorium. As a result, our fields were soon so overtaken by weeds that passersby couldn't even tell what we had planted.

Then one weekend fifty farmers showed up to our farm. Soon they were digging, bunching, sacking, loading, and sending the harvest of our field crops off to the packer. My parents were very grateful. Their thanks were met with this response: "You've been doing plenty to help all of us. It's our turn to help you."

This is community. I learned early that community means people working together to get done what would be very difficult or impossible for one or two persons alone. The practice of community was an essential part of life in the immigrants' home villages in Japan. It became more so in the communities where Japanese immigrants settled in America. Baseball, people gathering around a spiritual center, people helping each other, gave me vivid examples as a child of the importance of community and the way it is built and sustained.

Chapter Four

Mother Keeps the Family Together

After Pearl Harbor

Just days after the bombing of Pearl Harbor, two FBI agents came to our farmhouse on the Yakima Indian reservation. It was nighttime. Sternly, the agents told my father, "Come with us." The last thing I heard my father say was "let me put on my pants" before he disappeared into the dark with the agents.

When the war with Japan started, the FBI began rounding up Buddhist ministers, Japanese language teachers, martial arts instructors, editors of the Japanese ethnic press, and small business merchants up and down the West Coast. My father was none of these. But because he had no legal papers from entering the country and had supervised the construction of the auditorium annex to the Buddhist temple in Wapato, he too was considered a leader and a threat. He was first taken to the county jail in Yakima and then to the

Department of Justice camp in Fort Missoula, Montana.

For the next six months my 25-year-old mother struggled to keep her family of five children together. She began working for Mr. Truman, the farmer who took over the land we had been leasing from the Yakima reservation. At the time, we were farming with horses, but neither my mother nor I were big or strong enough to handle them. I was eight years old at the time. My youngest sibling was only two months old.

Before the war, in our farmhouse we had a calendar that had pictures of all the presidents of the United States. I remember how my father would tell me stories about each of the presidents and quiz me on their accomplishments on evenings after work. The presidents were all very real people to me, the type of people who deserved great respect, but who also felt like someone I could go to for help. Through the sharing of such stories, my parents conveyed to me the faith and hope they had in this country.

As the spring planting season approached, my mother suggested that I write to the President and tell him we needed to get our father back. President Roosevelt, of course, was leading the country in two wars across the Pacific and Atlantic oceans. Even though I wrote him the best letter I could, he had no time or interest in answering an eight-year-old boy.

Instead, he signed Executive Order 9066 authorizing all people of Japanese descent living within 200 miles of the Pacific Ocean to be confined in what he called concentration camps.

Ironically, when the orders came for the entire Japanese immigrant community to leave the Yakima Valley, we were first moved into the very Buddhist temple auditorium that my father had built. From there we were evacuated to the temporary camp set up at the Livestock Pavilion in Portland, Oregon. The Portland site was one of fifteen such temporary prisons. These were hastily organized and spread out from the county fairgrounds in Puyallup, Washington to the Santa Anita racetracks in Los Angeles County. The majority of the camps were in California's Central Valley.

Heart Mountain

After three months in the Portland Assembly Center, we were moved to a more permanent camp in Heart Mountain, Wyoming. There were ten of these prisons, euphemistically called relocation or internment camps. Once settled in Heart Mountain, my mother and I resumed our letter writing campaign. This time we wrote to Edward J. Ennis, Director of the Alien Enemy Control unit of the Department of Justice, asking him to release my father and have him rejoin our family. After a year of writing to Director Ennis, I received a letter addressed to "Master Isao Fujimoto," indicating that Ennis knew he was writing to a child. Ennis told me he would investigate my father's situation. In a subsequent letter to my mother he told us that my father would soon be released from the Fort Missoula, Montana detention center and would join us in Heart Mountain. We would still be imprisoned but at least we would be reunited as a family.

After hearing this news, my sister Yoshi wrote to my father and said, "I hope you'll be home soon. Plenty of room our place." Our place happened to be one room crammed with six of us within a barrack that housed five other families. Reading this letter not long ago, I was struck by my sister's sense of generosity. I realized that "plenty of room" had a broader meaning, reflecting a legacy passed on by my mother to her children. It was a statement of generosity, of making space for people in our hearts, and of how that space is more important than physical space.

My Mother's Faith

Years later, I thought back on what my mother and I had done. In particular I wondered what had allowed my mother to stay so calm and focused during such a harrowing time. I realized that her inner strength was based on the teachings of

Buddhism, specifically the Four Noble Truths and the Eight-Fold Path.

The Four Noble Truths state that:

- Suffering is a part of life;
- We need to understand the causes of any suffering;
- It's important to take action to resolve the suffering; and
- To end the suffering we must follow the Eight-Fold path.

The Eight-Fold path is an ancient guide to resolve suffering through: Right View, Right Intention, Right Speech, Right Action, Right Livelihood, Right Effort, Right Mindfulness, and Right Concentration. The latter three summarize the steps my mother took to get our father back.

Right Concentration includes practices such as meditation that help to calm the mind and emotions, avoid panic, allowing for Right Mindfulness and thinking. This paves the way for identifying the Right Effort needed. My mother calmly identified the steps we needed to take, encouraging my involvement, and continued to act until we found the solution to what was hurting us. Though she never had the opportunity to pursue higher education, or even finish high school, my mother's calm and focus was born from deep wisdom and a spiritual center that she drew from again and again over her long life.

Surprised by a Photo

On my 79th birthday my daughter Esumi gave me a copy of *The Great LIFE Photographers*, a compilation of some of the best LIFE magazine photos over a 75-year period. The photos of people, places, and events in the book are memorable and inspiring. Some photographers capture people and places identified with world changing events. Others depict everyday life in places all around the world. One I liked was of a first grade class in New York on a field trip to a nearby grocery store to buy lettuce for the class' pet turtle. Another was of a family of bushmen in South Africa enthralled in a story-telling session narrated by their wide-eyed, animated elder.

From the hundreds of pictures that were selected for inclusion in the volume, there was one that I was surprised to see and with which I identified completely. This was a photo taken during the winter in the midst of World War II. Hansel Mieth, an immigrant from Germany, took the photo. This was not a shot from the war theatres in the Pacific or Europe, however, but from a concentration camp in Heart Mountain, Wyoming.

The picture shows a crowd of people saluting the American flag on a cold December morning in

1943. A caption on the photo notes the temperature that morning was 18 degrees below zero. Surrounding the flagpole is a Boy Scout troop with its drum and bugle corps. All the uniformed scouts are people I know. I know their names, their families, where they lived and farmed before the start of the second World War.

I remember that cold morning, as I was also in the crowd. I was ten years old, a member of the Cub Scout Pack that was the companion to the Scout troop. We were all from the same place: Yakima Valley, Washington. All farming on the Yakima Indian reservation. All together now, for no just reason, in the Heart Mountain, Wyoming concentration camp.

Heart Mountain held 10,000 inmates parceled out into 30 blocks. Each block had two sections with 16 barracks in each section, which included a mess hall, laundry, toilets and boiler room that heated hot water for the mess hall and communal bathroom. Each barrack was partitioned into six rooms with a family in each room. Families with more than six members got two rooms. Once my father joined us, we were assigned to Block 15, Barrack 16, rooms E and F.

Tule Lake

We were soon moved to the camp at Tule Lake near the Oregon border. This was the beginning of my life in California. Of all the wartime camps that imprisoned those of Japanese descent, Tule Lake was the most controversial and contradictory. In 1943 all imprisoned adults were given a loyalty test. They were asked if they would serve in the U.S. military and if they would forswear allegiance to Japan. Those answering "no" or leaving the questions blank were declared disloyal. It didn't matter to the authorities that Japanese immigrants were ineligible for citizenship in the U.S. and that answering "yes" would have therefore left them without a country.

Tule Lake was designated as a segregation center to which all "disloyals" were sent. Family members in the camps who were U.S. born faced a dilemma. My mother, for example, was born in Seattle. But since our family had just been reunited, she answered "no" to both loyalty questions so we could stay together as a family.

Life in Tule Lake had many ironies. My school-age siblings and I went to Japanese school in the morning and American school in the afternoon. At the Japanese school, we would start the day bowing to the east. At the American school in the afternoon, we would begin by pledging allegiance to the American flag.

Another irony was the amount of free time we had at both Heart Mountain and Tule Lake. Before the war, youth from Japanese farm families went home right after school to help on the family farm. During the winter months, they went to Japanese language school instead. Involvement in extracurricular school and community activities was minimal. In the camps, however, we suddenly had the opportunity and time to participate in scouts, sports, and other youth programs.

When my father joined us in Heart Mountain, he brought with him numerous objects he had made during his own free time at Fort Missoula. One was an inkwell made of polished pebbles. Another was a rock on which he had painted a lady clad in a kimono. This rock, which fits into the palm of a hand, is featured on an entire page of a book entitled: *The Art of Gaman: The Arts and Crafts from the Japanese American Internment Camps, 1942-46*, compiled by Delphine Hirasuna. *Gaman* means "enduring the unbearable with patience and dignity."

When our family moved to the camp at Tule Lake, my father was called on once again for the good of his block community. While he was imprisoned at Fort Missoula, my father had not only channeled his artistic vision, he had also become a softball pitcher and had apparently was quite good.

So he literally pitched in to help out his new team at Tule Lake.

It was in the Tule Lake camp that my father gave me a life-changing gift. My father had noticed my interest in stamps. Seeing that I had little equipment, my father looked through a Sears Roebuck catalog and ordered me a stamp album. It was the biggest Scott's album available and it cost five dollars. As a cook in the prison camp, my father was paid sixteen dollars a month. He had invested nearly a third of his month's pay to get me that album!

The impact of that gift was liberating. As I studied the images on the stamps, my imagination flew me over the barbed wire to places all over the world. It was the beginning of my life-long quest to know about the amazing people who live on this planet, their languages, cultures and ways of life. It was no doubt the reason that many years later I became a rural sociologist working with people from all over the world to improve their lives and communities.

On the Close of Tule Lake

One final irony played out long after the camp was closed in 1946. The Tule Lake camp inmates, with their farming know-how, had turned the 3,000 acres surrounding the camp into productive farmland. Productivity was so high that crops were used not only to feed the Tule Lake camp population but shared with other camps as well. In fact, the conversion to productive land was so successful that the U.S. government declared the area a homesteading site for veterans after WWII. What did the veterans produce? Tule Lake became known as the "horseradish capital" of the world.

Horseradish, of course, is made into *wasabi*, the hot green condiment that accompanies sushi and sashimi, Japanese raw fish delicacies. At its peak, Tule Lake produced a third of the world's supply of horseradish, much of it exported to Japan. So here is the irony: a land made productive by people of Japanese descent, a people discriminated against because of their success in farming and imprisoned because of the war between Japan and America, became farmed by former soldiers who fought in the Pacific, and ended up producing an essential and well liked item in Japanese cuisine.

What I take from all these experiences is two-fold: a deep appreciation for my mother's strength and courage in keeping our family together; and the realization, nourished by my father, that our minds and spirits are far stronger than any barbed wire or unjust laws used to imprison us.

Redress, 43 Years Later

On August 10, 1988 I was invited to speak at a press conference at the California State Capitol on the occasion of President Ronald Reagan's signing of Redress for Japanese Americans and Aleuts imprisoned during the war. After telling the audience about my childhood letter to President Roosevelt, I went on to say the following:

> As a child in the camps, I knew something was terribly wrong but I lacked the words to describe my feelings or our situation. Years later I found the words: injustice and betrayal. I think of the pictures of the presidents on our wall and the promise of freedom and justice they seemed to offer. But my experience as a child showed me that the very people I trusted and respected – our country's leaders – didn't trust us or respect the fundamental rights due all of us. The very country we were taught to have faith in, didn't have faith in us.
>
> Today is an important day in the healing and growth of our country. Redress means the restoration of trust and faith in ourselves and in our country. Redress means we can trust our country, that our country is big enough and has heart enough to make amends to citizens it has wronged.
>
> By this decision on redress, America sends a vital message that no country is so big or powerful that it cannot own up to its

errors. Redress tells us that it's not "our country right or wrong." It is about being proud of country when it's right, and when it is wrong, we need to all work to make it right again. Redress is a victory for everyone because it reminds us that our country is guided by the principles of freedom and justice for all.

In camp, one phrase I heard often was "back home": how things were back home, if we would ever get back home again, and if not, where was home anyway. Long after the war, these questions of where we belonged haunted many of us. Redress means that for all of us who were sent away, we are finally back home again, at home in our country and at home with one another.

Chapter Five

Starting Over

Pleasanton, California

In December 1945, our family was released from the Tule Lake Segregation Center located near Newell, California. Tule Lake had held nearly 20,000 inmates of Japanese ancestry at its peak. The War Relocation Authority directed the resettlement process. Five thousand inmates were repatriated to Japan. Other families returned to their former home areas. But most – like my family – found themselves starting over in new communities spread across the country.

The Southern Pacific Railroad recruited workers like my father for its operations in the community of Pleasanton, California. The town was located in what we now call the Bay Area. It had a population of 3,000 and was surrounded by three military bases. My father was assigned to a work crew fixing railroad tracks. We were given fifty dollars and a ride on the train to Oakland, California. Our family, which had now expanded into one with six children, settled into one of Southern Pacific's section houses, a small space meant for couples.

I was filled with a mix of emotions. It was exciting to be out of the camp, free to explore, and settle in a new place. But there was also apprehension since we were the lone family of Japanese descent with school age children in a town filled with thousands of returning servicemen. Most of the soldiers and sailors I encountered made nothing of my presence. But one day I was confronted by a resident who angrily exclaimed: "Get out town, you Jap!" I was twelve years old then but the size of a Pleasanton fifth grader. Not only were the students in the Pleasanton elementary school bigger than students of comparable age from the camps, they were largely from families whose members and relatives had fought against the Japanese.

So it was with a sense of trepidation that I entered a seventh grade class in Pleasanton a few weeks before Christmas 1945. On the day before Christmas break, students exchanged gifts with classmates whose names they had previously drawn. After the last student was handed a present, a classmate plopped a huge package on my desk. It was full of school supplies purchased with a collection taken up by the class. Not having the money to purchase school supplies myself, I was surprised and grateful for this generous gift. Even more, I was reassured by my class' gift of welcome, friendship, and hope.

Due to my family's limited economic circumstances, I sought out opportunities to earn money for the family as a pre-teen. I discovered that the possibilities were numerous. I cleaned people's yards, shined shoes, and sold seeds and inspirational placards door to door. I also began to sell newspapers on the streets for the *Oakland Post Inquirer* and the *San Francisco Call Bulletin.*

When the Alameda County fairgrounds in Pleasanton opened for the horseracing season, I began hawking newspapers three times a day. Early in the morning I would sell at the stables where the owners and trainers were exercising their horses. I would return in the early afternoon after school to sell the edition, sought after by bettors, that carried the recommendations for each race. In the early evening, after the races were done, was when I hit the bars in town where the bettors gathered. I soon found it more lucrative to have my six year old brother, Kaz, enter the bars with an armload of papers than to do so myself. Just in tips alone, he would earn more than I made selling in the morning and afternoon combined.

In the process of all these activities, what fascinated me most was the variety of people that I encountered. Up until this point I had been surrounded – both in Yakima and in the concentration camps – mainly by people who were of Japanese descent. Now I was meeting people called white who went by a host of identities: Irish, Swedish, Russian, Italian, German, British, Danish, Portuguese, and on and on. This was one of my earliest lessons in the diversity of cultures, races, and ethnicities in California.

When spring arrived in 1946, a combination of circumstances led to another fruitful experience. In the camps, baseball had been a popular activity. It was more than a past time, it was a means by which community was built. Baseball brought people together. Something similar happened to me in Pleasanton. At Tule Lake I had played on both my school and block teams, and because we played often, my knowledge included game strategies as well as technical skills. When the Pleasanton Elementary School principal, who happened to be the baseball team's coach, saw me play, he pulled me off of the seventh grade team and put me on the more advanced team, comprised mainly of eighth graders. In addition to providing a path towards recognition and acceptance among my peers, baseball also turned out to be a way of breaking down barriers. Almost daily I had faced a very hostile school janitor, but when I scored a winning run against a rival school, things changed. He started bragging about my sportsmanship and his hostility was replaced by friendship.

Our family lived in Pleasanton for just ten months after our release from Tule Lake. Although I did not go on to high school in Pleasanton, as the former president of our eighth grade class I still receive regular invitations to rejoin my friends at reunions of their Amador Valley High School class. I go because my short stay in Pleasanton had a profound impact on my life. The friendship and kindness I experienced there taught me to live with confidence and good will, even in the midst of prejudice and difficult times.

A Book That Made A Difference

Dale Carnegie's book, *How to Win Friends and Influence People* also had a big impact on me at this time. I was curious about the very different people I was meeting in school and in town. A central theme of Carnegie's book was that the key to making friends involves being genuinely interested in others. As others can attest, this is a trait I have developed throughout my life. In fact, over the years my children have enjoyed mimicking how I meet and get to know people – whether on the subway, at a meeting, or at a social function. They laugh when doing these impersonations but I notice all three have become wonderful conversationalists.

Carnegie's suggestions on how to make friends were practical and quite helpful to me as a young person. He reminded his readers, for example, to appreciate and call every person by their name. For Carnegie, a person's name was the most important sound to that individual. Carnegie's advice was similar to what I had heard growing up in an ethnic Buddhist community. There was a common Japanese saying that is loosely translated as: "Work hard, respect others, and don't brag." In Carnegie's language this became: "Be a good listener. Encourage others to talk about themselves and their interests." Also important was Carnegie's instruction to "Look for the good in others. Find what makes every person interesting."

I put a lot of Carnegie's suggestions into practice. One of my assignments as student body president of Live Oak High School, for example, was to visit every elementary school's eighth grade class in the small towns that made up the school district. I talked with the incoming students about what to look forward to when they became a part of Live Oak High School. I included upbeat comments about the new experiences and friends they would be gaining. I always wrapped up my presentation by saying a good way to make a lot of great new friends was to "wear a smile and approach others by acting as a good friend yourself. " This came straight out of Carnegie's book!

Seeking Help From the ACLU

While I was out making new friends, going to school, and earning money, my mother continued to teach me how to stand up in the face of injustice. One day when my father was working on the railroad in Pleasanton, he called me over to the pile of gravel where he stood near the rail tracks. He told me to be prepared to help my mother run the family. I was twelve, he said, old enough to be "the man in the family," if necessary. My father had, unbeknownst to me, just received a notice that he would be deported back to Japan. He had come to America three years after the passage of the 1924 Anti-Oriental Exclusion Act that forbid immigration from Asia. As a result, my father was what we would call today an undocumented immigrant.

Our family's unity was threatened once again. This time my mother and I got on a Greyhound Bus to San Francisco and met with Wayne Collins of the American Civil Liberties Union. Collins was the attorney who defended Fred Korematsu, Gordon Hirabayashi and Minoru Yasui in their case before the U.S. Supreme Court. These three *Nisei* (first generation American born, of Japanese descent) had refused to go to camp and were arrested. They charged the U.S. government with violating their civil rights as American citizens. Initially, the ACLU and Korematsu, Hirabayashi and Yasui lost their case. The Supreme Court in a 6-3 vote ruled that the wartime internment was justified.

The Supreme Court's 1942 decision upholding the imprisonment, however, was based on an altered collection of documents supplied by the U.S. military. The military, which had pushed for the evacuation and incarceration of people of Japanese descent, had removed vital intelligence reports from their filings with the court. These documents argued that there was no military necessity that justified imprisoning 120,000 people of Japanese descent, the majority of whom were American citizens. Interestingly, it turned out that the missing documents from investigations led by the FBI and the Office of Naval Intelligence were written by Edward Ennis, the man who had orchestrated our family's reunion during the war.

Thankfully, Wayne Collins succeeded in staying my father's deportation. However, *Korematsu vs. United States* would not be overturned until 1983, when the Supreme Court declared that the incarceration of Japanese Americans during the war was "unconstitutional."

Sadly, we live in a time where that same case has been cited by some in Congress as being a good precedent for banning Muslims from our country. Fortunately, the Japanese American Citizens League (JACL) – of which I am a long-time member – and other groups are standing up to challenge this incendiary claim. In the meantime, the Fred T. Korematsu Elementary School in my hometown of Davis, celebrates the civil rights activism of Korematsu every year on his January 30th birthday.

My mother's efforts to stick to a goal – in this case it was once again to keep her family together – set a powerful example for me. She persisted and succeeded in spite of being ignored, imprisoned, and having to overcome one obstacle after another. Her display of perseverance got embedded in my subconscious. It's kept me going all my life.

Share Farming in Madrone

With the threat of deportation removed, it was time for my family to move on. When I was in eighth grade in Pleasanton, my father learned of an opportunity to get back into farming. Driscoll Strawberry Company in Santa Clara County arranged for us to begin share farming in the hamlet of Madrone, a town of about 300 people. Driscoll was keen to recruit families like us because Japanese immigrant farmers had a reputation for possessing a strong work ethic and great agricultural skills. We became one of fifty Japanese families working for Driscoll in Madrone.

In share farming, families were responsible for the care and harvesting of the crops while Driscoll managed the marketing. In high school by then, I was in charge of the family's accounts. One day looking over the bill of lading that summarized the prices we got on our crates of strawberries, I noticed vast differences in the prices received in sales to different companies. The price of an entire crate of 12 baskets, for example, was $3.00 if sold to Safeway in the 1940s. Those sold to Scatena brought only $1.27 for a crate. So why, we wondered, was Driscoll selling to Scatena when better prices were possible elsewhere? We learned that Driscoll had borrowed money from Scatena with the understanding that it then had to use their broker services.

In share farming, the farmer has no say in marketing, no way of getting the best price for their crops. This is the reason, after four years with Driscoll, many families – including ours – began renting land so we could start farming on our own. The productivity of independent Japanese American farmers once again resulted in bountiful crops. Unfortunately, at the peak of harvest, the prices for our strawberries would drop dramatically. This was because farmers were all harvesting and selling the fresh fruit at the same time. Our community of farm families responded by joining the Naturipe Strawberry Cooperative. In this way, the market for our fruit was expanded. Even more important, we were able to use the Co-op's freezer to package frozen strawberries. In addition, our strawberries were sold to ice cream and jam companies, freeing

Co-op members from being wholly dependent on the fresh fruit market.

An Observant Sister

Life in Madrone was not all work and school. My younger siblings were often a source of amusement. One of my favorite stories involves my sister Shoko who was six at the time. One day she found me reading *Ripley's Believe It or Not*.

Our conversation went something like this: "What are you reading?" asked Shoko. I replied: "I'm reading about some amazing ways people can turn a bad situation into a good one."

"Like what?" said Shoko.

"Well," I explained, "here's a man in China who was born with a hole in his head but he didn't cry about it."

"What did he do?" asked Shoko.

"He lived in a village that had no electricity or streetlights. But at night he could still walk around the village to check things out," I said.

"How did he do that?" I told her, "He lit a candle and put it in the hole in his head. This helped him see his way around at night."

"Oh," said Shoko, "I'm going to go outside and play now.

A few minutes later I discovered what Shoko had absorbed during our talk. The Yamaguchi family were in the barracks next to ours. When I stepped outside I heard my sister calling out to her friend: "Hey, Sachiko. Your little baby brother have a hole in his head so you could put a candle in it?" Sachiko thought for a minute and very politely answered: "Noooo."

I was very impressed by the exchange between the two six-year-olds. I was also reminded that young children take in what is going on around them. They are carefully watching how people, including their older brothers, behave. I resolved to remember this lesson and act considerately with everyone, regardless of their age.

The Power of Films

One of the first movies I watched after the end of World War II was *The Best Years of Our Lives*. It was about people trying to regain what the war had taken away. For Homer, who came home with hooks that replaced his arms, WWII took away part of his body. For Fred, returning to find his wife gone, his marriage was what war destroyed. For our family, it was our dream of America as a land of opportunity that was sorely damaged.

I identified with the film. The war had taken something away from all our lives. In our separate ways, we had to start over. We all had to rebuild. There would be ups and downs. The road would not be smooth. To get back up, we would have to work hard, work together, and help each other.

That's what each of the share farming families in the Driscoll camps did. These were also the stories of the main characters and families in *The Best Years of Our Lives.*

Recently I saw a Brazilian documentary called *Wasteland* that has inspired me in much the same way as *The Best Years of Our Lives.* It is a story about people making a living from Rio de Janeiro's *Jardim Gramacho*, the largest waste dump in the world. It, too, is a film about rebuilding, of making something out of what others have thrown away, in this case garbage. The film focuses on Vik Muniz, a Brooklyn based Brazilian born artist. Muniz uses scraps and throw-aways to create his art. Originally Muniz intended to create portraits of *catadores* – garbage pickers – who sort through tons of waste each day to get items to recycle and sell. Once he got to know the spirit and energy of the people, however, he changed his mind and had the *catadores* create their own self-portraits. These large photographic canvasses have now been seen and celebrated in art galleries around the world.

Not long after learning about the making of *Wasteland*, I heard about *Cateura*, a film named for a dump outside of Asuncion, the capitol of Paraguay. In Cateura, the garbage pickers pick out items from the waste that some of them turn into musical instruments. Children in schools and neighborhoods near the dump have become proficient performers on these instruments made from trash. With the guidance of a musical director, the children now have an orchestra aptly named Landfill Harmonic.

These three films – *The Best Years of Our Lives*, *Wasteland,* and *Cateura* – are all about rising above destruction be it by war and/or poverty. The stories all emphasize the need to harness creative energy to rebuild lives and community. They are stories of the human spirit's power to turn despair into hope. They are also my family's story – and those of many Japanese Americans incarcerated during the war – of starting over in a country that was torn then – and is torn now – by forces of xenophobia, racism and oppression. Kindness, cooperation, and community are what allowed my family to begin again and thrive. In reviving their dreams, my family and many others – then and today – keep alive the hope of an America that welcomes, cares for, and acts justly for all people.

Chapter Six

Going Out Into the World

Off to College

In the fall of 1951, I left home to start my studies at UC Berkeley. I walked from our strawberry farm to the old U.S. Highway 101 running through Coyote, California. I stood on the shoulder of the highway and flagged down a Greyhound bus. That took me to San Jose where I transferred to a Berkeley-bound bus. After I was let off near University and San Pablo Avenues, I started flagging down buses going towards campus. Not a single bus would stop.

So I kept walking until I came upon a group of people. They looked like they were waiting for a parade. When I asked what parade was coming, I got this answer: "We're not waiting for a parade, we're waiting for a bus." In all the previous places I had lived, there were no public buses except school buses that stopped in unmarked places where students would wait. I asked how much it cost to get to campus. The reply was "25 cents." I had earned money for college by taking on various jobs in addition to my work on the family farm. One job involved irrigating 50 acres of cucumbers. Pay for farm work in the late 1940s was 75 cents an hour. Since I was already a third of the way to Cloyne Court Co-op on Ridge Road where I would be living and knew I would have to be frugal, I kept walking.

Cal turned out to be a life-expanding shock. We had moved to Coyote to start farming the year I started college. The road marker claimed Coyote's population at the time was 150. Since I am the eldest of thirteen siblings, our family constituted ten percent of the small farming community south of San Jose. My first class at UC Berkeley was Chemistry 1A, which had an enrollment of 300 students, double the number of people who lived in my entire hometown! Here were students from all over the state filling up the seats in just one big classroom! Amazing! And so was everything else.

I soon discovered that every building at Cal was comparable to a community the size of Coyote and more. So each week I explored a different part of campus. One week it would be Hearst Mining with its collection of minerals from around the world. The next week would take me to Life Sciences with its endless cases crammed with pickled specimens. Still another excursion would be to Anthropology with its displays showing how Ishi, the last man in his tribe, survived. In addition to visiting buildings, I read bulletin boards posted around structures such as the library, offices of student organizations, the *Daily Cal* and the gym. These provided a treasure trove of information and nudged me from the ethnic cocoon of my childhood into a vast new world.

The students at UC Berkeley were another source of fascination. On my first work shift at the Co-op's Central Kitchen on Oxford Street, my working partner introduced himself saying, "I am Hazum Al Tak from Iraq. I am an Arab!" Getting to know people like Hazum, from places I had known only through the stamps I collected as a child, was exciting. So it was with everything I encountered in college. Not just the classes – the whole campus, the students at Cal, and the multitude of choices for involvement was enriching.

It certainly worked for me. Being on the judo and wrestling teams; participating at Stiles Hall; helping out a local Scout troop; meeting people like Alan Watts and Gary Snyder at seminars at the Berkeley Buddhist church; and making contact with the student movement in Indonesia as part of the Cal Indo team were all part of my UC Berkeley experience.

I started at Cal after graduating from Live Oak High School in Morgan Hill. Our school teams were called the Acorns. I went off to UC Berkeley as if I was an acorn, and Cal provided me with the nutrients necessary to grow into something much, much bigger.

The Cal Indo Project

The Cal Indo Project became one of my favorite activities. Students like myself were invited to meetings with faculty, graduate students, and a visiting scholar from the newly formed country of Indonesia. Formerly the Dutch East Indies, this was another place I first got to know through the stamps I collected in the concentration camps. Through the Cal Indo project I was soon taking classes on Bahasa Indonesia and attending meetings on the challenges facing the new nation.

In 1954 UC Berkeley selected a group to make contact with the Indonesian student movement. Our task was to initiate projects between the university and Gadja Madja University in Central Java. Our team of six consisted of the political science professor Robert Scalapino and five students. One of the graduate students was studying architecture and he was tasked with the design of a student union building at Gadja Mahda. A junior at the time, I was appointed chair of the delegation.

My participation with the Cal Indo Project was world- and mind-expanding. It also led to numerous other invitations and experiences. One of our team members, for example, was active with

World University Service (WUS) which raised funds to assist students and universities struggling in the aftermath of WWII. He invited me to join him at the gathering of WUS representatives in England. It would be my first time in another country.

Between the meeting at Oxford and the gathering of the Cal Indo team in Singapore, I decided to hitchhike around Western Europe. What moved me most as I travelled through Europe were the people I met and the experiences they shared. Among these was a former German soldier I met in a Quaker work camp. He asked me about the city of Oakland, California. After being released as a prisoner of war in Russia, he had returned home and was surprised to learn his wife was living in Oakland. Never hearing anything from or about him, she had assumed her husband was dead. She went on to marry an American soldier and had resettled in California. When she learned her first husband was alive, she wrote to him. How did he react? The former German soldier told me: "I got many letters from her. I didn't open a single one. I burnt them all."

I remember, too, the kindness of people like the former French soldiers of Vietnamese descent who took me to Versailles. Another time, I found myself buoyed by the hopeful outlook of German orphans with whom I shared a room in a youth hostel. I was also caught up in the enthusiasm of other young people who had just returned from a visit with Albert Schweitzer on the Bodensee in Switzerland. Youth from throughout Western Europe revered Schweitzer, who had dedicated his life as a medical missionary in Lambarene, Gabon, and who was now in Europe to deliver his belated acceptance speech for the Nobel Peace Prize that was awarded to him in 1952.

The Crying Man

An occurrence with a more ominous foreboding unfolded on my flight to Calcutta. An Asian man sitting next to me was crying. When his sobs eased, I asked him if I could get him anything. He thanked me and asked me where I was going. I answered, then quietly asked what was bothering him. He replied, "A terrible decision was made. I am now going home to a country that has been split into two."

This was August 1954. With the defeat of the French at Dien Bien Phu earlier in the year, Vietnam had shed its colonized past. However, the future of the newly liberated country was not for the people of Vietnam to decide. With a global ideological battle raging between Western nations and the Communist bloc, major world powers had a vested interest on which side Vietnam would join. Representatives of the great powers – West and Communist – met in Switzerland and drew up the

Geneva Accords. The agreement called for the division of Vietnam into a Communist aligned north and a Western oriented south. The Vietnamese included Ho Chi Minh who signed the Accords. Tran Van Do, a physician and Foreign Minister from the south of Vietnam, refused to sign the Accords. Tran Van Do was the crying man sitting next to me on the flight to Calcutta. The tears shed by Tran Van Do that day foretold the great suffering that would befall not just the Vietnamese but also thousands of families in America.

Working with Indonesian Student Leaders

The post World War II world was changing in dramatic ways, with new countries emerging from former colonies throughout Africa and Asia. The transition from colony to country had been violent in Indonesia. Many of the student leaders we met had fought against the Dutch. Backed by the Ford Foundation, our Cal Indo Project focused on identifying their needs and priorities through discussions with leaders of various student organizations. We spent the majority of our time at Gadja Mahda University in Djokjakarta in Central Java. Our efforts there included the design of a student union building, the identification of books needed to bolster library collections, and the development of a student exchange program between Gadja Mahda and UC Berkeley.

After our work was completed at Gadja Mahda, our team split into two. One group stayed for extensive discussions with organizations in Jakarta. The other group, my own team, traveled the length of Sumatra by bus. Midway through Sumatra, in the town of Padang Sidinpuan, word of our presence got around. Two former Japanese soldiers came to see me. They were part of a contingent of the Japanese army that had chosen to join in the Indonesian fight for independence rather than returning to Japan. Given the scarcity of food and other difficulties facing Japan after its defeat in WWII, these former soldiers had decided to start their lives over in a brand new country.

Upon my return to Berkeley, I met with Chancellor Clark Kerr, reporting on the highlights of the Cal Indo Project's activities and accomplishments. Soon I was busy accepting invitations to speak at numerous groups in Berkeley and the Bay Area. The Cal Indo Project eventually led to training and exchange programs, creating a bond between students from UC Berkeley and Indonesia.

Medical School

Prior to my trip to Indonesia, I had been accepted into medical school at the University of California, San Francisco. Classes were already underway when I returned. But I felt out of sync, and not just because I had missed out on the beginning of a new semester. I had a gnawing sense that I was destined for fields other than medicine. My intense summer experiences in Europe and Indonesia had revealed to me previously unknown possibilities.

I found it hard to concentrate on my classes in anatomy, physiology, and biochemistry. I was going through the motions but not doing well. At the conclusion of my first year of medical school, two faculty members met with me to report that my performance did not warrant my continuing.

With the medical school door now firmly closed, I began to flounder. I reached out to Thomas C. Blaisdell, a professor in the School of Business Administration. He, along with professor of Economics, Professor Condliff, and Chancellor Kerr, were on the committee that selected the Cal Indo team. I told Professor Blaisdell about my first year at medical school, acknowledging that I was at a crossroads in my life, and in need of advice. He recognized my dilemma at once and invited me to meet him for lunch at the UC Berkeley faculty club.

Professor Blaisdell's supportive approach made me feel at ease. Instead of dwelling on my setback, he suggested that I view what happened as a message to redirect my energy. He then proceeded to share his own experiences of dropping out of college.

As an undergraduate at Columbia, Blaisdell was struggling and questioning the value of continuing with his studies. Instead of continuing at Columbia, unhappy and without purpose, he took the year off and went to teach In India. There he found a renewed sense of purpose and returned to finish his undergraduate career at Columbia before going on to graduate school. But in graduate school, Blaisdell found himself again questioning the value of what he was doing. He dropped out of graduate school and went to teach in China. Later, he returned to Columbia yet again and completed his Ph.D. In the ensuing years, Blaisdell became well known for his academic work at UC Berkeley, including his two business administration specialties: India and China.

Blaisdell told me it was time to follow my instincts. He said that while my calling might not be clear yet, I should follow what felt right and seek new opportunities. In doing so, he assured me, my path would appear. I left our meeting feeling both reassured and uplifted.

Thomas Blaisdell entered my life for only a short period but his impact has been profound. He put me on a path that continued to open up my world. He gave me helpful suggestions so I could craft a vision of my future. We all need people in our lives whose insights and guidance recharge our sense of purpose. Thomas Blaisdell did that for me.

He was a remarkable friend and made a huge difference in my life.

Returning Home to Work

After receiving my Bachelor of Arts degree from UC Berkeley in Biological Sciences, I went home to the Santa Clara Valley. I coached Little League baseball while helping the family on our strawberry farm. One day a group of parents who had sons on the baseball team approached me about applying to be the principal teacher at Machado, a one-room public school on the outskirts of Morgan Hill. I had never considered teaching but after an encouraging interview for the position I enrolled in several education courses at San Jose State. In the end, the school district picked someone else for the position – someone who had the requisite teaching degree. But I was enthused enough about the possibility of teaching to enroll at San Jose State full-time so I, too, could get a teaching degree.

In the meantime, I needed to earn some money. In the fall of 1955, while I attended classes at San Jose State, I saw a posting for a deputy probation officer position at the Hillcrest Juvenile Hall in San Mateo County. The job involved working with juveniles who were awaiting disposition of their cases. The youths' violations ranged from being runaways to committing assaults and robbery.

At the interview I was hit with a series of questions. The chief probation officer seemed bent on discouraging me from taking the position. Towards the end of the interview, he asked me curtly, "You'll be eating lunch with the kids. One will yell out, 'Pass the fucking butter.' What would you do?"

"I'd pass the butter," I replied.

"Is that it?"

"Sure. With a group like this, making a big deal about   table manners can backfire,"

"What did you do at Berkeley besides study?" the Chief asked me, intrigued.

"I was on the Cal wrestling and judo teams," I said.

The Chief looked at me and asked, "When can you start?"

Once on the job, the reason for the Chief's line of questioning became clear. All the other probation officers I met were big men. I am 5"4' and weighed 120 pounds, both then and now. Most probation officers were police majors as well as athletes, either football players or judo competitors at San Jose State.

But it turned out it didn't matter what size I was, where I went to college or what my major had been. What mattered was if I could break up fights or handle situations before they got wildly out of control. It turned out I could. I later did my student teaching in the juvenile hall. One of the guidelines at the hall that surprised my supervisor from San Jose State was the rule that forbade the use of pencils, since they were objects that could easily be turned into weapons.

Sputnik

I was a U.S. Army correspondent in Korea when the Soviet Union launched Sputnik in 1957. When I returned to California, I found people scared and asking: "What do we have to do to beat the Russians?" One immediate answer was: "We need to beef up our high school science programs." In response to Sputnik, universities throughout the country set up summer and yearlong institutes to retrain high school science teachers. Their goals included starting classes in the New Math, offering three different approaches to teaching Biology, and making major revisions in the teaching of Chemistry and Physics.

After my military service as a U.S. Army correspondent in Korea, I started teaching chemistry and biology at San Jose High School in San Jose, California. I was inundated with brochures on Institutes to attend. At that time San Jose was the key city in a fruit growing area known as "The Valley of Garden Delight." Today the same place has been redubbed "The Silicon Valley."

While Sputnik fired up a revolutionary pace on space science in the United States, there was a simultaneous revolution happening on the ground. This was the civil rights movement. Civil rights struck me as equally vital to the U.S. as getting to the moon. As a result I looked for a science teacher training offered by a predominantly Black university where I could focus on both issues: science and the appalling poverty and racism in the country.

Howard University

I was accepted at an Institute for Radiation Biology at Howard University in Washington, D.C. With the exception of two nuns from Chicago, all of my colleagues were African Americans teaching in segregated schools in the deep South. Learning about their lives and daily experiences educated me about the challenges and opportunities facing our nation. One colleague was a former All American football player at Langston Hughes College in Oklahoma. I asked him how he got to Washington, D.C. He mentioned connecting with another participant from Texas with whom he drove non-stop to D.C. with a large grocery bag filled with peanut butter sandwiches to eat in the car. I asked why they had driven non-stop. He said that they had stopped at a gas station to use the restroom but "The attendant told us, 'There's one for you guys over there but it's busted.'" He went on, "If the guy didn't like us, we knew he could have framed us for rape. We just let it go and left."

I asked another classmate how he got into teaching high school. He explained that after graduating from a historically Black university in Alabama, he was left with two choices: he could either take the exam to become an employee of the Post Office or he could apply for a teaching job at a segregated school for Black students He chose the latter.

Another chemistry teacher told me he recycled litmus paper. These bits of paper used for determining if a liquid is acid or a base were throwaways in California schools. But my Institute colleague did not have enough litmus paper for his students. He also had very limited lab equipment and greatly outdated textbooks. Nonetheless, this man claimed he was better off than many other Black teachers who had to teach science classes with no lab at all. These and similar conversations made me realize we had as much distance to travel in human relations as scientists were attempting to traverse in space.

Cornell

The year following my return to San Jose, I was accepted into the one-year Institute for Biology located in the College of Agriculture at Cornell University. I have Sputnik to thank for bringing me to Ithaca. While there, I was invited to assist with a Cornell literacy program in Honduras, a country where 70% of the population was illiterate. In the summer of 1962, I led a team of Cornell students to the village of Santa Rita de Yoro to teach adults how to read and write in Spanish. When I returned from Central America, I thanked the San Jose Unified School District in California. Then I told them of my decision to stay at Cornell to work on a Ph.D. in Rural Sociology. Without my hands-on experiences in Honduras, I could not have taken this step.

My doctoral studies at Cornell were made possible by a job teaching a lab section in Biology and free housing at Telluride. The latter provided not only much needed material support, but also exceptional opportunities to meet with other students and faculty. Frances Perkins, former Secretary of Labor in President Franklin D. Roosevelt's administration, was then a professor in Cornell's School of Industrial and Labor Relations. She also served as a faculty member in residence at Telluride. Telluride hosted numerous activities such as seminars and receptions for visiting

64

speakers. For a seminar on the New Deal, Perkins succeeded in getting two other former members of FDR's cabinet to join her in Ithaca: James Farley, Postmaster General, and Henry Wallace, Secretary of Agriculture and later Vice President during Roosevelt's administration.

Several Telluride residents were excited about working in countries outside the U.S. and asked Wallace what fields and training would best prepare them for international work. Wallace answered, "Know one thing really well and that will take you all over the world." For Wallace that thing had been corn. Later, after he left government service, Wallace retired to a farm in New York where he concentrated on breeding various plants, especially strawberries.

At the Telluride gathering, I got a glimpse of how Wallace could focus on knowing "one thing, really well" – in this case, strawberries. When he learned that my family farmed strawberries, he asked me to join him for breakfast to discuss how we grew and marketed the fruit. Several months later, Wallace surprised my parents by sending a representative to my family's farm in Morgan Hill, California so he could learn more about our production of strawberries.

As I followed Wallace around later, his single mindedness was evident. After meeting Peter Hopcroft, a Cornell student from Kenya, Wallace turned the conversation to strawberries. He asked my friend if he had noticed what kind of strawberries were growing at particular elevations on Mt. Kilimanjaro.

A similar exchange occurred with Mrs. Einaudi, wife of Cornell professor Mario Einaudi, whose father Luigi was the second president of the Republic of Italy. Wallace asked Mrs. Einaudi if she had ever been on Mt. Etna. When she said yes, he immediately followed up, asking her if she had seen any strawberries growing there.

My years at Cornell coincided with the tumultuous events of the 1960s. In August 1963 I was among the 250,000 people at the March on Washington to protest racial injustice. I went with a contingent from Cornell, spending most of the bus ride from Ithaca, New York to Washington, D.C. conversing with Paul Wolfowitz, a fellow resident at Telluride. Paul was a math major. He was idealistic and personable. Later this same Paul Wolfowitz would go on to become the architect of the Gulf War. I have often wondered what caused my friend to take this particular path in his life, knowing that all of us are changed – albeit in different ways – by the events taking place around us.

Tragedy Strikes

In 1964 my brother Kaz was serving in Korea as a photographer with the U.S. Army. I was in the

Philippines doing fieldwork on village development for my dissertation. My sister Yoshi was running a carnation nursery in Morgan Hill; my sister Toyo was working in New York. We were all called home when a drunk driver killed three of our siblings: Keiko, Shoko, and Donald. They had been riding in the family's Volkswagen minibus on a sightseeing visit to San Francisco. With them, were my other five siblings – Tomiko, Shigeko, Janet, Annie, Coleen, and Motoko – and Christian Rappaport, a home-stay visitor from France. When my parents were told the devastating news, they rushed to San Francisco, having to go from hospital to hospital to find their injured children.

The deaths of Keiko, Shoko, and Donald were a stunning loss for all of us. Keiko and Shoko had been living together in Berkeley. While Keiko worked in the university's library, having just graduated from UC Riverside, Shoko attended City College of San Francisco. Donald was a junior at Live Oak High School in Morgan Hill. Because these three occupied the middle spot between their older siblings and younger ones, they were the ones most conversant in both Japanese and English and therefore played a critical role in the family.

At the time of their deaths, the family had a large unpaid mortgage on the land we had purchased in Morgan Hill. My father fell into a deep depression, affecting his ability to farm. Concurrently, the price of strawberries, the family farm's primary crop, had dropped astronomically. As a result, my family was in a very precarious situation emotionally and financially.

But after the funeral, an insurance agent appeared at our house. She had read about the tragedy in the Bay Area newspapers. She informed the family that Keiko, a young woman in her early twenties at the time, had taken out a life insurance policy designating our parents as the beneficiary. Keiko's investment enabled our parents to pay off the mortgage on the farm. The proceeds from Keiko's unexpected generosity also gave our parents and family a valuable reprieve and time for us to bounce back – to rebuild our lives – once again.

In 1966 I finished my Ph.D. fieldwork on village development as part of the University of Philippines–Cornell Project. But before I could finish my dissertation, UC Davis came calling. Along with my first wife, Linda Wilson, I packed my bags and headed west.

Chapter 7

University of California, Davis

A Rousing Start

I came to the University of California, Davis in the spring of 1967 eager and ready to work with the newly formed Department of Applied Behavioral Sciences in the College of Agriculture. Trained as a rural sociologist at Cornell, I took to heart the call inscribed on UC Berkeley's Hilgard Hall: "To rescue for human society the native values of rural life." However, I was to learn there's more to the academic world than the producing and sharing of knowledge. In any endeavor – be it business, government, farming, or higher education – participants line up on various sides of any issue. In a university setting, which supposedly champions objectivity and fair evaluation of different points of view, there still lurks the real possibility of having to face the question: "Whose side are you on?"

In order to get a better sense of the context in which I would be designing and teaching courses on community development, I embarked upon a tour of California's Central Valley, the richest agricultural region in the entire world. It is also home to some of California's most impoverished cities and towns. In the first of what would become countless trips to the Valley, I met with groups such as the American Friends Service Committee (AFSC) and the United Farm Workers (UFW). The AFSC ran projects in community action, social justice and rural development. I met with family farmers and workers at their office in Visalia . The farmworkers were two years into their strike for better wages and working conditions in the grape fields around Delano. I joined them in their strike at Guimarra Vineyards.

Not long after I returned to Davis from my visits in the Central Valley, I got a call from Pancho Botelho, a UFW organizer in the Yuba City-Marysville area. The call was both urgent and short:

"We have a problem. Can you help us?" Pancho asked.

"What is the problem?" I replied.

Pancho explained, "The school board has stopped bus service to the migrant labor camp. Our children now have to get to school by walking along Highway 99. It's very dangerous."

"Give me a couple of days to see what kind of resources we have and I'll get back to you," I said.

There were no taxis or public transportation in Davis at that time. But UC Davis had some creative student leaders who were establishing a bus service. Instead of going local, student leaders Bob Black, then Student Body President, and Richard Klecker called across the Atlantic Ocean and arranged for the purchase of a dozen used London double decker buses. In addition, they arranged for a mechanic to come with the buses to get them ready for operation in Davis.

I called Bob Black, who would later become mayor of Davis, and explained the request from the UFW organizer. I asked if a bus might be made available to transport the farmworkers' children to school and back. Black was very supportive and sent Bud Johnson, a newly hired bus driver, to meet with me. Bud asked for someone to go to the Valley with him to watch out for the low hanging wires along a route off the major highway.

Glen Burch, director of University Extension at UC Davis, was involved in training Peace Corps volunteers slated for Nepal when I first arrived on campus. He was enthused about my starting courses in community development and asked if there was anything he could do to help me. I told him it would be useful to have a teaching assistant as I began the new courses and program. He approved the funds and hired Molly Freeman, a graduate student in Sociology, to be my assistant. I asked Molly if she would be willing to go with Bud Johnson on the bus to get the farmworkers' children to school. She responded enthusiastically: "Of course!"

A red double decker bus with its "Buckingham Palace" destination placard still in place could not remain incognito for very long in the Valley. Molly was soon invited to appear on a local Yuba City radio show to explain the appearance of the bus in their area. Molly told the audience that the bus was there to help children from a migrant labor camp get safely to and from school after their bus service was suddenly cut.

The reaction that followed was explosive. Large growers in the Yuba City area called UCD Chancellor Mrak asking what a University-identified bus was doing helping out farmworkers' children. To placate the growers, Mrak ordered Molly Freeman to be fired. Glen Burch reluctantly did so. Instead of going off quietly, however, Molly organized a picket around the UCD administration building. Her fellow students marched with Molly, carrying signs that declared, "University research and services should serve ALL people."

A debate soon followed. Over one hundred faculty members, most from the College of Agriculture, gathered to hear three speakers. One was Roy Bainer, the chair of the Department of Agricultural Engineering. His department had recently developed the mechanical tomato harvester. The other speakers were Molly Freeman and I.

The agricultural press covered the event, praising Bainer and UCD for its advances like the tomato harvester. Molly and I acknowledged the importance of such technical innovations in our presentations. However, we also pointed out the importance of examining the social impact of such technology. The tomato harvester, for example, did not just reduce the labor force. It also changed the work force composition. Sorters on the harvester became predominantly female and were paid less than their male counterparts. Also, plant breeders were encouraged to develop "harder" and more "square" tomatoes so the claws of the new harvesting devices would not bruise them. No concern was given to how those hard, square tomatoes would actually taste or be received by consumers.

Molly and I – and those who supported us - were accused of wanting to hold back progress. One director of Agricultural Extension was so incensed he sent me a letter saying that I was *persona non grata,"* or in other words, I was not welcome in his county. Molly left UC Davis shortly thereafter and got her Ph.D. in Complex Systems Analysis from Union Institute and University. These days, in addition to preparing educators for online learning environments, Molly continues her activism with the Jewish Alliance for Peace and Justice, a group seeking the peaceful coexistence of Palestine and Israel.

This all happened in my first year at UC Davis. Besides getting me off to a rousing start, this experience awakened me to aspects of the academic world I had not been told about. Some terms such as "farm labor" were clearly more than research topics. They carried with them political implications. So responding to a request for assistance from a farmworkers' representative meant being seen as "on the other side." Sending the tall London bus to Yuba City was not seen as an effort to keep children safe. Instead, it was interpreted as a political act supporting farmworkers. Being red in color no doubt added to the supposed political message carried by the bus.

The farmworker movement continues to be a strong advocate today for those who grow and process California's abundant vegetables and fruits. Recent accomplishments include the passage of a law granting farmworkers overtime and environmental regulations to ensure the safety and health of farmworkers and their children.

The year 2016 marks the 50-year anniversary of the Delano Grape Strike. What is usually overlooked – or unknown – is the multi-ethnic involvement in that historic event. The strike was initiated by the Filipino Agricultural Workers

Organizing Committee (AWOC) with the Mexican National Farm Workers Association (NFWA), the union of which was later manifested in its re-naming as the United Farm Workers (UFW).

The languages used in the first grape strike are also noteworthy. Workers' signs were not only in Tagalog, Spanish, and English. There were also signs in Arabic, hoisted by workers from Yemen. During this period, there were some 7,000 men flown from Aden in the Arabian Peninsula to Stockton, California. This cultural diversity and wealth are subjects that I continue to raise whenever I speak about the Central Valley.

Working from Home

With the atmosphere on campus so charged in the late 1960s and 1970s, I found it more conducive to do most of my work at home. I only recently have come to realize it was because I so often felt unwelcome on campus. As a result, my home soon became a popular meeting place for students engaged in newly emerging topics such as safe food, alternative energy, organic farming, family farming, and community action. At one point, five organizations had their offices on my back porch: the Alternative Agricultural Resources Center directed by Janet Mercurio, the International Tree Crop Association headed by Henry Esbenshade and Miles Merwin, and the Rural Resources Access Project (RRAP).

Students who worked with me included Martin Barnes and Henry Esbenshade who helped start the Davis Farmers Market. Ann Evans, later mayor of Davis, was also one of my assistants. Ann oversaw the Davis Food Co-op from its initial household membership days to its current status as a major Davis food market. Other students were actively involved in helping start the local organic farm association and the annual Ecological Farming Conference.

Today these former students are respected leaders in their communities and in their fields. The institutions they founded in Davis are now celebrated parts of the city. Red double decker buses continue to take people of all ages around town. Names and movements that were once reviled in 1967 are no longer so, such as the former West Davis Elementary School located only one hundred yards from my home, now renamed Caesar Chavez Elementary, which offers a full K-6 Spanish Immersion Program.

As with the red bus, the hive of energy at my home did not go unnoticed. Students living in and associated with my house began putting into practice organic gardening and energy conservation. Before long we were producing eggs, herbs, fruits and vegetables. We were also raising honeybees and chickens, and had replaced the front lawn with a miniature fruit orchard.

Not all of our neighbors appreciated our efforts. We learned that one neighbor who lived behind our back yard was allergic to bees. So our four hives were reduced to zero. The chickens – a rarity in Davis neighborhoods at the time – bothered a couple who lived nearby. They told us that when our chickens laid their eggs in the early morning, their loud cackles startled their cat, who would jump on the husband, causing him to roll over in bed, swinging an arm that would wake his wife. Angered by having her sleep disrupted – again – she would pick up the phone and call our house, yelling, "Shut up those chickens!"

There were also regular potlucks and meetings of people involved with the various organizations based in the house, as well as a steady stream of visitors who came to view the projects or access materials in the Alternative Resources Center. When a community college bus brought a group of students to visit the house, a neighbor on Linden Lane filed a complaint to the Davis Planning Commission. What followed was a special session of the Planning Commission to appraise the situation. The meeting included a slide show of the projects associated with the house and presentations by both the concerned neighbors and residents of 870 Linden Lane. Neighbors shared their concerns about the increase of traffic in a residential block and also with the impact on property values when one resident replaces a front lawn with fruit trees and a garden. Today, of course, after a five-year drought, a number of our neighbors have also done away with their front lawns.

The Planning Commission was cordial, thanking everyone for their participation. The Commission chair encouraged the 870 Linden Lane residents to reach out to all our neighbors. We did so by giving the neighbors a tour and reception, listening to their concerns, and answering questions. It helped that the majority of Planning Commission members were former students of mine who recognized that the activities at 870 Linden Lane were innovative and consistent with the emerging identity of Davis.

ABS 47.

Over my fifty years at UC Davis I have taught many classes. One of my most popular has been ABS 47. Here is how the course worked:

Students would gather before 8 a.m. on a Sunday, shivering and sleepy, as my assistants directed them to the vans that would take them to San Francisco. For the next four days these thirty UC Davis students would spend part of their winter break taking a class called "ABS 47: Urban Community Resources." They would see a part of

San Francisco that most had never glimpsed before, including those who grew up in the city. They would also be initiated into an experiential way of learning shared by more than 1,000 students involved in ABS 47 over the 30 years I taught the course.

Prior to our departure one December morning, I wrote to each student describing the course and the orientation they were required to attend: *"Welcome to ABS 47, our class on Urban Community Resources. Our class is an intense four-day field course where we will be going from morning until late evening each day. We'll be living together in a hotel in San Francisco's inner city, sharing rooms and making contact with more than 20 organizations in different parts of the city."*

No matter what students had heard about the class – at orientation or through friends – their days were a series of revelations. One of their first stops in San Francisco was Glide Memorial Church where students attended a high energy, multimedia, gospel singing worship service. Afterwards, they talked with church members, program participants, and staff about the congregation's housing and recovery programs for those who were homeless and/or addicted. Later in the week students would serve long lines of the hungry at St. Martin de Porres' soup kitchen.

During the class small groups of students visited neighborhood organizations across the city from Chinatown to Haight Ashbury, south of Market to the Mission. They talked with sex workers, gay activists, and former prisoners turning their lives around at Delancey Street. Students sat on the sidewalk with those who were homeless, walked the streets of the Tenderloin with a Night Minister, went out with the Mobile Assistance Program, and met with city officials and urban planners.

Just as important, the class learned how to operate as a community and look out for each other. Students engaged in team building exercises, talked in small groups, wrote in their journals, and made friends with people they would have ignored or maybe even made fun of on campus.

One of the skills I taught students in this class and others was called "Front & Back." Through an urban scavenger hunt, I encouraged students to sharpen their perceptions by looking at what is in the back of the city, a neighborhood or a street. The Tenderloin section of San Francisco, for example, borders Market Street and is close to the Financial District. But given the large numbers of low-income people and service centers for the homeless and destitute, the larger public usually avoids the area. In this way the Tenderloin becomes the back stage, while downtown serves as the city's front stage.

Students reacted to this experiential type of learning in a variety of ways. Some were shocked by what they saw and would have preferred to stick their heads into a book about homelessness. Some couldn't wait to get back to Davis and their own rooms and circles of friends. But the majority of students embraced the experience, rightly seeing it as an adventure, a rare opportunity to learn by doing. Each time I taught the class, I could see students gaining confidence and compassion. I watched as they shared a sandwich or gave away their coat to someone living on the streets. I listened as they raised new questions: questions about what is fair and just, questions about what keeps people stuck, questions about what they wanted to do with their lives after graduation. Some students even changed their major as a result of the class. Or began volunteering with organizations on campus or in the Sacramento region. Many expanded their previously classroom-focused education and started taking new risks, doing things they never thought they could, as they became a more visible, active part of their communities.

Friendships forged over the four-day course continue, sometimes for years. Our potluck reunions – with slide shows – let us all relive the highlights of our time together. Some of the students became assistants, developing leadership skills and sharing responsibility for the success of subsequent classes. Thanks to social media, students often stay in touch with their ABS 47 classmates, as well as with me. They return for Picnic Day, ask for recommendation letters, and enjoy talking about how the class has affected their lives and, often, their work.

The students are not the only ones who are changed by this experience. Each of my children – Caedmon, Basho and Esumi - have participated more than once in ABS 47. Their ease around people different from them, people who might be homeless or mentally ill, immigrants or felons, stems from these early experiences.

I have been changed too. ABS 47 became a living laboratory in which I could experiment with the way I teach. The lessons I learned found their way into the work I do in the larger community, across the country and across the Pacific. This is the kind of teaching that brings us together, makes a difference in the world, and makes learning a lifelong pleasure.

Summer Abroad

A few years before retiring, I started a UC Summer Abroad class called "Community & Everyday Life in Japan," at Ryukoku, a Buddhist University in Kyoto, Japan. Yoshio Kawamura, a former classmate at Cornell, friend, and professor at

Ryukoku, was instrumental in making this class possible. From 1991 to 2013, over 500 UC students from Davis, Los Angeles, Berkeley, Irvine and other campuses participated. Each was paired with a Ryukoku University student called a "tutor."

As was true of my earlier classes on the Davis campus, especially ABS 47, learning was experiential. Students did not simply sit in a classroom taking notes on lectures. Instead, they met with a variety of Japanese activists and organizations working on issues from homelessness to discrimination against the *burakumin* (an outcast group), historic preservation to sustainable farming, women's rights to suicide among youths. They also explored life in Kyoto, hiking to mountain top temples, attending the Gion Festival, and visiting villages specializing in ceramics and other industries. Many of these students have continued to be in contact with one another, their Japanese tutors, and me over the years. Some have gone back to Japan to teach or have pursued careers shaped by their experiences there.

It was a special pleasure to have my children Basho and Esumi, and my grandson Bela Buson, accompany me to Japan during some of those summers. By the time she was eleven, Esumi was a class veteran, taking part in class field trips, talking with students and reading their work, even counseling a mother who flew to Japan to be with her son after he was hospitalized for a serious illness. In later years, when Esumi was a college student herself at New York University, UC Davis hired her to be the local on-site coordinator. Her responsibilities included organizing field trips, taking students to the doctor when they fell ill, grading their papers, and mediating student conflicts. Even though Esumi was younger than most students in the class, they quickly came to respect and depend on her.

Basho played a similar role and was also hired by UC Davis at times. In 2009, the H1N1 virus (also known as swine flu) hit Japan hard. The UC students were quarantined in their dorm for over a week after a Ryukoku baseball player was diagnosed with the flu. Basho did a great job of keeping the students calm, leading them in yoga exercises, organizing games, and encouraging them to work on their projects. Meanwhile, Basho's son – Bela Buson – kept the students laughing and well stocked with snacks.

It became my practice at the end of each UC Summer Abroad session, to meet with village development trainees at the Asian Rural Institute (ARI) in Naoshiobara, Tochigi in northern Japan. Esumi joined me on many of those visits. The ARI provides a year's course on agricultural and village development for community workers from Africa, South Asia, and South Pacific. On each visit I gave talks and shared experiences on community and agricultural development in California and the U.S. I also had them share the sounds animals in their country made -- building on my experience from my elementary school days. In addition to great hilarity, such practices contributed to students' appreciation of each other's cultures.

Teaching & Building Community

I often asked my students, "Who was the best teacher you had and why?' Being in a University environment, it is not surprising that the best teachers are often remembered with comments like "he really knew his stuff;" "she wrote the definitive textbook;" and "they are number one in their field." Others identified good technique as the mark of their best teacher: "best speaker I ever heard;" "always clear in explaining;" "had great examples and visuals that made everything easier to understand." It is noteworthy, however, that such responses usually made up only a third of the comments received.

What is it that defines a teacher besides being knowledgeable or having great teaching methods? The answers came from students remembering the relationship they had with certain teachers, be they elementary or high school teachers, coaches, music instructors, or even family members. The students' comments were revealing: "She said I was special;"

"I was a slob but he never gave up on me;" "I was told I could be great but I needed to keep improving and so he kept giving me challenging assignments;" "We were poor and my teacher bought the first suit I ever owned so I could be dressed like everyone else for my graduation." In other words, these teachers were saying, "I care about you." In doing so they provided the human connection that is critical for inspired learning to take place and community to be built.

It has been a privilege teaching at a place like UC Davis filled with so many bright, eager, energetic young people not to mention talented staff and faculty. But it is important to remember that being smart is not enough. There are plenty of smart people in the world. Not all of them are up to good. Look at the front page of the morning's paper and we'll see stories about smart people doing some pretty bad things: lying, cheating, stealing, destroying people's lives. Few of these stories are about people involved with the mafia. Instead, they are often stories about people running churches, corporations, or governments.

So a good strategy for those of us facing a roomful of smart, talented students is not to ask them, over and over again, to demonstrate how knowledgeable they are. Rather, we need to challenge every student with questions like these: "What are you going to do with your gifts and talents? How can you use your gifts and talents to build community no matter what you do, where you go?" A good University may have a Nobel laureate or two. A great University creates a community in which smart, caring people can thrive and make a difference in the world. For all the struggles and criticism I endured at times, I have known such a community here – at UC Davis - and am glad to have contributed to it

Chapter Eight

Work in the Community & World

The Power of a Gift

It was close to Christmas 1943. My father was still in the Department of Justice camp in Missoula, Montana while the rest of us – five kids and our mother – were in the Heart Mountain, Wyoming camp. As I was walking back to our room in Block 15, some teenage girls called out: "We have presents for your family." I wondered who could be sending us presents as everyone we knew was locked up in camp. Besides, we didn't celebrate Christmas. So I shouted back, "Where did they come from?" They answered, "They're from the outside."

"Outside" referred to non-Japanese people not imprisoned inside the camp. I looked for clues as to the senders of the packages and found names but few addresses: there were no rural routes, PO boxes or street numbers, just the names of small towns in places like Nebraska and Iowa. The return address on my package read, "American Friends Service Committee." I didn't know who these people were at the time, but in the forthcoming years I continued to learn more and more about their good work relocating *Nisei* college students from the camps into colleges back East and helping former internees during the difficult resettlement period after the war.

Fifteen years later in 1958, after I had finished my military service as a U.S. Army correspondent and had started teaching Chemistry and English at San Jose High School in San Jose, California, I visited the Northern California office of the American Friends Service Committee (AFSC), then located on Sutter Street in San Francisco's Japantown. I thanked the staff person I met there for the sweater I had received as a young boy and for the assistance the AFSC had extended to the Japanese American community in a time of great need. I added that I was ready to give back. This was to be the start of a life-long association with the AFSC.

The person I spoke with that day was Karen Handwerg, secretary of the AFSC's High School Program. When I offered to help, Karen, learning of my tie to San Jose High, started me off by inviting me to join their High School committee. Our work included organizing social justice conferences at Asilomar in Pacific Grove, California. These annual conferences attracted several hundred high school students from all over Northern California and featured such stalwarts as Harry Ashmore, editor of the *Arkansas Gazette,* and Martin Luther King, Jr.

When I joined the faculty at UC Davis to start its community development program, I worked with a progression of other AFSC committees including: Farm Labor, Family Farms, Asian Pacific, and the Executive Committee. My last assignment was as the Pacific Mountain Regional Office's representative to the National Affirmative Action Committee, which held its meetings in the AFSC's central office in Philadelphia.

Arriving early for a National Affirmative Action meeting, I asked for permission to explore the archives that occupied a big part of the basement floor. I stopped to examine file boxes marked "Student Relocation Program." When I looked through the boxes I was struck by the number of letters written on behalf of just one Japanese American college student for whom the AFSC was seeking release from the concentration camp in which he had been interned. The Student Relocation Committee wrote not only to the college where the student had been accepted, but also to various townspeople where the college was located: the Chamber of Commerce, veterans' organizations, local school principals, church leaders, and so on. Each letter asked for their support in welcoming a student whose education had been disrupted by circumstances of the war.

The AFSC succeeded in placing close to 4,000 students in over 680 colleges in the Midwest, Great

Lakes, and New England areas, far away from the Pacific Coast war zone from which their families had been forcibly removed. On average about twenty-five letters were written on behalf of each student. Or, in other words, almost 100,000 letters total were written in the days before computers and photocopiers. What I saw in the file boxes was the result of time-consuming work done using typewriters, carbon paper duplicates and mimeograph machines.

Ongaeshi: Repaying Debt with Gratitude

How do you thank people who come to help you with such meticulous care and kindness? The beneficiaries of the National Student Relocation Program figured out a way. Japanese culture recognizes that when people do something for you, an obligatory reciprocity is created, and you are expected to respond to their gesture with gratitude. In Japanese, "*on*" is the word for obligation and the act of responding to *on* with gratitude is called "*ongaeshi*." Beneficiaries of the National Japanese American Student Relocation Council expressed *ongaeshi* by creating the Nisei Student Relocation Commemorative Fund (NCSF).

In 1980 a group of Asian Americans involved with the AFSC met in Seattle to discuss the challenges facing the various communities of people of Asian descent, especially with the arrival of refugees from Southeast Asia. That's when I met Lafayette Noda, formerly from the Livingston Cortez community. After the meeting, Noda returned to Dartmouth and convened a group of Nisei beneficiaries of the wartime student relocation program now living in New England. Recognizing how much the AFSC had helped them when they were uprooted, the organizers of the Commemorative Fund decided to focus their attention on Southeast Asian youth. For just like the Japanese Americans, these youth and their families were going through the trauma of displacement during a time of war.

Since 1983, the NSCF has awarded half a million dollars in scholarships to 600 students from Southeast Asian refugee families and has built an endowment of over $650,000. Award ceremonies have been held in target communities where refugees settled, from New England to the Great Lakes, Texas to California. The awards have gone to distinct ethnic groups in specific locales in California such as Cambodians in Long Beach, Vietnamese in San Jose, and Hmong and Mien in Merced. The spirit of its motto conveys the NSCF's active practice of *ongaeshi*: "Extending helping hands once offered to us." It is a motto I have tried to embody in my life as well.

National Center for Appropriate Technology

As questions about tenure swirled around me in the late 1970's, I decided to take a leave of absence from UC Davis and serve as the Associate Director of the National Center for Appropriate Technology (NCAT) in Butte, Montana. I began working with groups across the country who engaged with low-income communities to lower their energy bills, start community gardens, and promote the use of alternative technology (e.g., solar ovens). My work and travels on behalf of NCAT gave me a national perspective and allowed me to connect with some outstanding activist groups like the Federation of Southern Cooperatives in Epes, Alabama, the National Sharecroppers Fund in North Carolina and the Highlander Center in Tennessee.

I was delighted to share my year in Butte with my son Caedmon. A fifth grader, Caedmon attended the local school and participated in a Boy Scouts troop that year. He also accompanied me on trips all over the country, allowing him to witness everyday life in low-income communities in the South and meet with activists in the civil rights movement. The characters we encountered during that time remain topics for dinner conversation today. Later, Caedmon's younger brother, Basho, joined us on a memorable raft trip down the Missouri River with our friends from Butte.

The aims of NCAT tied in well with the energy savings programs started by some of my students in Davis. In fact, as I worked on a community energy plan for NCAT I was asked to get a document called the "Davis Energy Plan" from my hometown. With Mayor Bob Black's assistance, I was able to purchase 1,000 copies of the plan, which were then sent to Community Action Agencies across the country as part of the War on Poverty.

When I returned to Davis, I mentioned to friends the unique role Davis was playing in the nationwide alternative energy movement. Out of curiosity, I asked a contact where they would send a visitor looking for information on alternative energy and appropriate technology. They replied: 870 Linden Lane – my home! For me, this underscored the importance of always looking in one's own backyard.

Rural Development Leadership Network

Over the last 30 years I have also worked with another amazing organization: the Rural Development Leadership Network (RDLN). This group works with rural leaders of color across the country, giving them an opportunity to develop new skills, network, and gain academic credentials through Antioch College.

The program began offering a month-long summer RDLN Institute at UC Davis in 1985. As a faculty member for the Institute, I taught a course called "An Overview of Rural America." This was, of course, a highly experiential, interactive class. I guided students on field trips through Davis and the Central Valley where they met small family farmers, cooperative leaders, civil rights and environmental activists, and university and government leaders. The students shared the challenges they faced in their communities and brainstormed possible solutions. Each student was then asked to undertake a project focusing on a particular issue of great concern to his or her community.

On alternate years, the group offered RDLN Assemblies, where we met students on their home turf, getting to know their communities and see their work up close. Here are two of the RDLN participants I have been fortunate to know:

Birgil Kills Straight is a Lakota elder from the Sioux nation in South Dakota. In 1986, a year after being a part of the first RDLN Institute at UC Davis, Kills Straight organized and led the Big Foot Memorial Ride. This two-week horseback ride traces the 300 mile journey of Big Foot, who led his tribe in a search for refuge after 150 of their kin were massacred by the U.S. Seventh Cavalry at Wounded Knee in 1890. Started to repair broken spirits, the Memorial Ride continues today as a way to foster leadership skills among Sioux youth.

Shirley Sherrod, another RDLN participant, was appointed by the U.S. Department of Agriculture to head the Georgia State Department of Rural Development. Her father was a Black farmer murdered by a neighboring white farmer. Instead of fleeing north, Shirley stayed to work on ways of improving the lives of farmers, both Black and white, in the South. A few years ago, Sherrod gave a public speech that was later misstated by Andrew Breitbart who accused her of refusing to work with white farmers. As Breitbart's blog went viral, the USDA fired Sherrod. Roger Spencer, a white farmer Sherrod had helped, came to her defense. The USDA apologized and offered her another position. Sherrod declined and instead wrote and published a powerful book called *Courage to Hope: How I Stood Up to the Politics of Fear.* She now serves on RDLN's Board.

My work with these and other dedicated activists has broadened my understanding of the challenges – and possibilities – facing rural America today. RDLN was also indirectly responsible for motivating me to pick up my long abandoned dissertation work. As I saw RDLN participants work to secure the academic degrees they had put aside because of the needs of their families and communities, I realized I could – and should – do the same.

Central Valley Partnership

I have long recognized that it isn't necessary to go far to experience the diversity in the world. The Central Valley has also been part of my backyard. During my travels up and down the Valley I have met farmworkers from Mexico, dairy farmers from Portugal, immigrants from Liberia, among others. My learning about the cultural diversity and wealth of the Central Valley intensified after my retirement in 1995 when I became the project facilitator for the Central Valley Partnership (CVP). From 1996 to 2006, I oversaw the work of 20 activist organizations and 150 emerging immigrant community groups. Sponsored by the James Irvine Foundation, these organizations stretched across eighteen counties in the Central Valley from Mt. Shasta in the north to the Tehachapi Pass in the south.

Most of the people in the CVP had never met or worked with people from other ethnic and immigrant groups. As they did so, the Partners discovered they had much in common, including: poverty, discrimination, concerns about safety, education, and their youth, and a desire to have a greater say in their lives and community. By working together they created new opportunities for all of them. They also came to appreciate and respect their differences and to share their "cultural capital" with one another and their surrounding communities.

The activist organizations brought a wide range of approaches to community organizing and action. These included the peace church and faith-based approaches of the American Friends Service Committee (AFSC) and Catholic Charities; Paulo Freire's liberation theology practiced by Fresno's *El Colegio Popular*; and the Sacramento Valley Organizing Committee's (SVOC) emphasis on applying pressure to holders of political power. The SVOC is an offshoot of community organizer Saul Alinsky's Industrial Areas Foundation.

As mentioned earlier, California's Central Valley is a place of great contrasts and contradictions. It is not just the richest agricultural region in California, but is the richest agricultural region in the United States, and the entire world. Yet the majority of the state's poorest cities and towns are also located in the Central Valley. Before the CVP, activist organizations attempting to address these contradictions were often stymied because they were isolated or worked alone. The James Irvine Foundation offered support – monetary and technical – to bring these activist groups together.

My role was to organize meetings that offered the Partners skills and opportunities to work together. But first we had to help the Partners to get to know one another, to build rapport and trust. This meant travelling up and down the Valley like circuit riders, meeting Partners in their communities, encouraging them to tell their stories and to listen to those of others. It also involved hosting meetings and events where Partners set goals and worked on specific projects.

For example, an early joint effort revolved around preserving a provision in the immigration law that permitted families with a mix of documented and undocumented members to stay together as a unit. Elimination of this provision would have led to families being broken up and some members deported. Another joint effort involved an appeal to the Regents of the University of California to permit qualified undocumented graduates of California high schools to enroll in the UC system without being charged out-of-state tuition fees.

The overall purpose of the CVP was to assist emerging immigrant organizations in becoming visible, active members of their communities. While the James Irvine Foundation initially focused its attention on promoting citizenship, the Partnership took a more flexible approach that recognized there were other paths for promoting active civic participation as well. The CVP, for example, set up a grant system that allocated funds for projects

100

considered priorities by the emerging immigrant groups. Some identified youth programs or the development of leadership skills as being most important to their communities. Other groups worked on immigrant rights and sought to make existing community institutions and agencies (e.g., police, job training, etc.) more responsive to the needs of immigrants in their midst.

One of the Partnership's greatest strength was its ethnic and cultural diversity. California's farm labor force has had a visible ethnic stamp from the very beginning of agricultural development in the state. Initially, for example, farm workers were Chinese followed by the Japanese. Punjabis from India and Filipinos were next. During the Depression, Dust Bowl refugees were a visible addition to the labor force.

Now the most visible farm workers come from Mexico and Central America. Contrary to popular perceptions, these people identify themselves not as "Mexicans" but by distinct ethnic markers. This becomes apparent in the variety of languages they use. We now have, for example, thousands of workers from the state of Oaxaca, home to 16 distinct ethnic groups. Mixtec speakers from Oaxaca are dominant in the Central Valley. Zapotec, Triqui, Chatino and Mixe are concentrated in other agricultural regions in California such as Napa and Salinas.

Other ethnic groups have played key roles in the introduction and/or production of particular agricultural commodities in the Central Valley. Armenians, for instance, are credited with introducing raisin grapes. Sikh farmers from the Punjab region of India grow half of all canning peaches produced for California in the Yuba City-Marysville area. Portuguese speaking dairy farmers from the Azores have made the Central Valley the number one milk producing area in the United States. Besides sharing a common ethnic heritage, the dairy farmers of Azorean background are further unified around islands of origin. For example, dairymen from the Azorean island of Texceira have relocated to San Joaquin and Tulare Counties. Those who trace their lineage to the island of San Jorge have gone to Merced County while dairymen from Pico are most numerous in Kings County.

County fairs have had a significant role in showcasing the Central Valley's agricultural bounty. Several of these fairs are now also the locales for ethnic festivals. During the December-January holiday period three cities – Fresno, Merced, and Sacramento - host festivals run by people from Laos. These festivals celebrate the Hmong, the most numerous of Laotians who have settled in the Valley. Other ethnic groups from Laos in the Valley include the Khmu, Lahu, Mien, and lowland

Laotians. Additional emerging organizations affiliated with the Partnership I worked with included immigrants from Russia, Cambodia, and El Salvador.

One of the Partnership's most popular and well-attended events is its annual Tamejavi Festival. The word "Tamejavi" is comprised of parts of three different words: *taj laj tshau puam* (Hmong); *mercado* (Spanish); and *nun javi* (Mixteco). Tamejavi was conceived as a space where diverse cultures could converge to express and share their stories, music, food traditions, and ways of interpreting the world. As the festival's organizers noted, "We need Tamejavi because it (1) Offers a medium through which immigrants express themselves and voice their ideas; (2) Builds new relationships and understanding among immigrants and long-standing residents in the Valley; and (3) Opens a public space that enhances expressions of creativity to stimulate a sense of belonging and promote community diversity." (www.tamejavi.org)

Finishing my Ph.D.

My work with the Central Valley Partnership during the first decade of my retirement also allowed me to complete something I had put aside during the early difficult years at UC Davis, namely: my dissertation. The insights gleaned from the Partnership's decade long efforts – instead of my long ago work in Philippine villages – became the subject of my new dissertation: "Dynamic Mosaic: The Central Valley Partnership's Collaborative Multi-ethnic Approach to Organizing Immigrant Communities." There was a certain satisfaction in successfully "defending" my dissertation at the end of my career, in 2010, rather than at the beginning. My reconstituted dissertation committee even included the son of my initial Ph.D. advisor.

At my family's urging, I agreed to participate in Cornell's graduation that spring. As news about my degree spread, I was invited to serve as the degree marshal for the procession of students entering Schoellkopf Stadium. When the ceremony organizers found out I was 76 years old, they suggested I could wait at the entrance of the stadium in lieu of marching the entire way across campus. I reassured them that regularly biking to the UC Davis campus for the past half-century had kept me fit enough to walk the distance. Besides, the procession was a short distance compared to the 50 years I had traveled to complete my Ph.D.

Cornell's President at the time, David J. Skorton, said in his commencement address: "Dr. Fujimoto is senior lecturer emeritus at the University of California, Davis, who completed his Ph.D. this year – 50 years after he put his dissertation on hold to begin an academic career working in rural sociology, farm labor issues, ethnic studies, social justice, and community, immigration and labor organizing."

The Nichi Bei Times was more succinct with its cover story of the event: "NEVER TOO LATE: Community Activist and Educator Isao Fujimoto receives Ph.D. from Cornell at age 76." While my parents were no longer alive to see me graduate, I know I would never have made it to that moment without their support and perseverance.

The spirit of my life's journey is captured in this poem called "Ithaka" written more than a century ago by Constantine Cavafy:

As you set out for Ithaka
hope your road is a long one,
full of adventure, full of discovery.
Laistrygonians, Cyclops,
angry Poseidon – don't be afraid of them
you'll never find things like that on your way
as long as you keep your thoughts raised high,
as long as a rare excitement
stirs your spirit and your body.
Laistrygonians, Cyclops,
wild Poseidon – you won't encounter them
unless you bring them along inside your soul,
unless your soul sets them up in front of you.

Hope your road is a long one.
May there be many summer mornings when,

with what pleasure, what joy,
you enter harbours you're seeing for the first time:
may you stop at Phoenician trading stations
to buy fine things,
mother of pearl and coral, amber and ebony,
sensual perfumes of every kind –
as many sensual perfumes as you can;
and may you visit many Egyptian cities
to learn and go on learning from their scholars.

Keep Ithaka always in your mind.
Arriving there is what you're destined for.
But don't hurry the journey at all.
Better if it lasts for years,
so you're old by the time you reach the island,
wealthy with all you've gained on the way,
not expecting Ithaka to make you rich.

Ithaka gave you the marvelous journey.
Without her you wouldn't have set out.
She has nothing left to give you now.
And if you find her poor,
Ithaka won't have fooled you.
Wise as you will have become, so full of experience,
you'll have understood by then
what these Ithakas mean.

Chapter Nine

Gratitude

Hotaru no Hikari
Mado no Yuki
Fumiyomu Tsukihi Kasanetsutsu
Itsushika Toshi mo Suginotu
Akete Zokesa wa Wakareyuku

Lights from a firefly
snow at the window
studying for days and months
years have rapidly gone by
now it is time to part
and go our separate ways

A Favorite Song

My mother's favorite song was "Hotaru no Hikari" (Japanese words and translation above). It is a song whose melody would be familiar to many since it is set to the tune of "Auld Lang Syne," a Scottish song sung at New Year's. But the words have a different meaning.

The firefly and the snow refer to a Chinese story about a poor, hard-working scholar preparing for a job in the imperial court. Because he could not afford candles or oil for a lamp, in the summer he would study under the light of the fireflies. In the winter, he would sit by the window to catch the light formed by the moon reflecting on the snow. So the song is about working hard, learning together, not giving up and then having to part and go separate ways. This is why the song is a popular refrain at Japanese graduation ceremonies.

This song describes beautifully Mama's life with us. She was a kind, wise, and thoughtful mother, a caring friend, and a wonderful partner for our father. My mother didn't have the chance for much formal education, but she made up for it by her keen interest in everything that her thirteen children were learning. She had a remarkable memory. Her curiosity about the world was fulfilled by her travels and the many visitors, local and international, brought home by her children. On being asked where or when she would like to travel, her response was, "Any place, okay. Ready, anytime."

When it came to providing support, love, and encouragement, Mama was always present. Whatever was needed – be it a clean pair of socks, a slice of apple pie, or a bus trip to the ACLU to get my father's deportation notice rescinded – my mother was always "ready, anytime."

Making Time for Family & Friends

I am grateful to have reached the age of 83. As I said when a dormitory at UC Davis was named for me in 2002, it is a great feeling to be alive – not dead – when given such an honor! It could have been otherwise. In 1991 I began experiencing a sore throat when I biked to campus. None of the doctors I consulted could figure out the problem until I went to an ear, nose, and throat specialist. He knew that a sore throat – due to the vagus nerve – could signal a serious heart problem. He immediately arranged for me to see a cardiologist at the UC Davis Medical Center in Sacramento. By late afternoon I was calling my wife, Christine, to tell her I would be having a quadruple bypass the next morning. That evening we had a nurse in my hospital room witness the signing of our will.

Luckily, I survived the surgery and did very well. I was back riding my bike and going off to do research in Micronesia six months later. In the years since my surgery, I have had a whole new life: the start of the Summer Abroad classes in Japan, the birth of my daughter Esumi, retirement, my work with the Central Valley Partnership, the birth of my three grandchildren - Bela Buson, Kodo, and Ruby - and the completion of my Ph.D., to name just a few.

Bonnie Ware, an Australian nurse and author of *Inspiration and Chai,* has had many talks with dying patients. She reports that among the regrets mentioned most often by dying people is not having kept in touch with their friends or family. I consider myself fortunate to still be in contact with students and friends that span 70 years or more. When I attend *Haru Matsuri* (Spring festival) at the Morgan Hill Buddhist Church, for example – where my sister Yoshi and her husband Tad are members, just as my parents were – I meet classmates from elementary school as well as my siblings and cousins.

Reunions are one of my favorite ways to reconnect and find out what has happened to old friends. In 1973, thirty years after our forced evacuation, I helped organize a reunion of returnees in the Yakima Valley. Listed on long rolls of butcher paper were the names of every resident who had been interned in a concentration camp during WWII. Participants at the gathering added names of spouses, children, occupations, and where they were currently living. After getting information from the families who did not attend the reunion, we were able to publish a directory listing three generations of names.

The reunion and compilation of the directory revealed that only twenty percent of the Yakima families who had been incarcerated during the war returned to the Yakima Valley to live and work. The majority of former Yakima Valley Japanese families were no longer farming. Many of the *Nisei* – or

American born, second generation Japanese – had gone on to college and to work in business, education and the professions because of their relocation to urban centers like Seattle, Los Angeles, Chicago, Detroit, and New York. Also striking were the names of the *Sansei* (third generation Americans of Japanese descent): Western names like David, Michelle, and Tom replaced common Japanese names like Tadao, Sachiko, and Yuri used in earlier generations.

Many of those who were placed in the camps never talked about their experiences. There was too much trauma, loss and stigma.   Often, third generation family members had no idea what had happened to their grandparents and parents until they started learning about the camps in college or met an elder willing to break the silence. As a result, it was forty years before the first Tule Lake camp reunion was organized. Subsequent reunions have included the slide show I made about Tule Lake, furniture and art work created in the camp, oral histories, camp newspapers, and photographs.

Today the Japanese American Citizens League (JACL) sponsors pilgrimages to some of the former camps – such as Manzanar – to help people of different ages, faiths, and ethnic backgrounds learn what happened there and what we must do to prevent such injustice from ever occurring again. After my daughter and I attended a Manzanar pilgrimage together, Esumi was invited to serve on the local organizing committee the following year. She was a high school student at the time. Committee members included *Nisei* who had been interned in the camp, JACL activists, and Muslim students and religious leaders involved with the Council on American-Islamic Relations (CAIR). It was clear then, and more so now, that today's rampant Islamophobia, violence, and acts of hatred towards the Muslim American community are frighteningly similar to what Japanese Americans experienced prior to WWII.

I enjoy meeting up with old friends and making new ones wherever I go. Other reunions that have rekindled and expanded my friendship circles have included those of Live Oak High School where I served as the student body president; Cloyne Court Co-op and Cal-Indo Project at UC Berkeley; San Jose High School where I taught Chemistry and English; Cornell's Honduras Project and Rural Sociology Department; and gatherings of students and activists in Davis.

Being the eldest of thirteen – now greatly expanded by the birth of children, marriages, and more children – makes for large, festive, noisy reunions as well. One Thanksgiving my sister Janet exclaimed, "This is the first family gathering I've gone to where we had to use name tags!"

Our family New Year's gatherings are a very special time of coming together. We cook and eat *ozoni* soup and red beans, traditional New Year's foods my mother used to make. Then it is time to dig into countless platters of sushi, teriyaki chicken, tempura shrimp, *mochi* (sticky rice cakes) and my sister Annie's colorful finger Jell-O. Since we are now multi-ethnic, multi-cultural, and multi-generational, there are also tamales, pasta salads, beer, and chocolates.

We used to make the *mochi* ourselves under my parents' supervision: first, pounding the steaming rice outside with long bamboo poles and mallets; then, shaping the *mochi* into balls filled with azuki bean paste. Nowadays, we make the *mochi* with a machine or purchase it from a local Japanese group.

In recent years the younger generation – many married with children – have begun hosting this highly anticipated gathering. While some watch football, others play with the kids, catch up on news of siblings and cousins, and hold the babies born in the past year. On the walls are photographs taken by each family along with family members' hopes for the coming year. Before the family disperses there is, of course, a group photo, usually outside which takes long minutes to organize. There is lots of laughter and squeezing close, as at least a dozen cameras are used to record the moment.

Lessons Learned

While I probably don't tell them enough (not bragging or bringing attention to a person being a strong Japanese virtue), I love and am immensely proud of my children and grandchildren. I hope they – as well as their cousins – will find value in this account of our family and my life.

In sum, here are the most important lessons I have learned over the course of my life and am still learning.

<u>Be True to Your Self</u>. While it can help to listen to others and seek their counsel, ultimately we must follow our passions and live our own life, not do the bidding of others. My parents stayed in farming all their lives. But they never expected any of their children to stay on the family farm. Instead, they encouraged each of us to get a good education and discover our own paths.

<u>Take Time Off</u>. Although farm work demanded a lot of our family's time, this didn't mean we worked non-stop. My parents recognized the importance of setting aside time for family activities outside of work. They were intentional about balancing work with opportunities for rest, hobbies and fun activities.

I remember an evening when we were still sharecropping strawberries with Driscoll. We were living in the small community of Madrone and there were seven children in the family then. After the harvest season slowed down, we all got into the car and my father drove us to a drive-in theater near San Jose. This was a first time experience for all of us. I don't remember much about the movie but I recall with fondness the cozy feeling of all of us sitting in the car, munching popcorn, and enjoying being together as a family.

<u>Stay Connected</u>. The importance of staying connected as a family also applies to other relatives and friends. Moments of reaching out, especially in times of need, are long remembered. When WWII was over, my father heard that his two younger brothers had survived their conscription in the Japanese Army. But he also knew the country was devastated by the war and people were hurting from lack of food, medicine and supplies. Upon our release from Tule Lake, my father joined a section crew repairing the tracks for the Southern Pacific Railroad Company. From my father's hourly wage of 67 cents an hour, my parents set aside funds to send monthly packages to family in Japan. The shipments included clothing, foodstuffs, aspirin and saccharin (a valued sweetener).

When I began teaching the UC Summer Abroad course in Kyoto, I would visit my cousins

Takeiku, Yoshiya and Haruo in Tachibana, near Osaka. Reminiscing about our family, Takeiku spoke of the packages they received from California while Japan was reeling from the effects of WWII. He recounted how overjoyed he was after receiving a shirt in one such package, remarking how special the shirt was because it had two pockets. Even though this had occurred nearly seven decades earlier, his gratitude remained strong and fresh.

Our cousins and their families in Japan have, in turn, opened their homes and hearts to us, showering us with *omiage* (gifts), preparing delicious and elaborate meals for us in their restaurant, and inviting us to stay in their home in *Esumi-mura*. My daughter Esumi and I have made more than twelve pilgrimages to *Esumi-mura* as a result of their hospitality. Caedmon, Basho and some of their cousins have also visited the village, poured water over our family's gravestones in the village cemetery, and stayed in Takeiku and Mieko's beautiful tatami floored house.

Even more significantly, our cousins and their families were there for us when my sister Toyoko lost her beloved daughter Mayumi to a sudden brain aneurysm and, later, when Toyoko developed Parkinson's disease. For many years, my siblings and I – and some of our children – have gone back and forth to Japan to take turns caring for Toyo in her home and, in her last year, the hospital.

We are especially grateful for the kindness and care showed Toyo by Masayo and her husband Kei. Masayo often visited Toyo in a skilled nursing facility. Masayo's foot rubs, treats and conversation, including visits to the cemetery to bring "reports" to Toyo from her late husband Yoichiro, brightened our sister's life in immeasurable ways and comforted those of us living far away.

<u>Get to Know the World</u>. The travels and experiences we have shared together as a family – in Japan, England, Europe, Ireland and in the U.S. - have brought me much joy and satisfaction. Watching my children and grandchildren travel on their own to new places like Mexico, Denmark, Costa Rica, Ghana, Jamaica, Turkey, and Mallorca is a delight. I am always happy to hear their stories about new people, new cultures, new languages, and new ways of being in the world. I hope these travels – whether far away or in places like California's Central Valley, Los Angeles, and New York – will continue to ignite their curiosity and give them a sense of the freedom and possibility I felt as a young man.

I hope my children and grandchildren will also consider going on trips together – with cousins and other family members - if possible. Following in my parents' footsteps, I took my younger sisters and brothers all over the country: from the segregated South to Indian reservations; from small towns like

Butte, Montana to big cities like New York and Washington, D.C. The adventures – and occasional mishaps - we shared were fun and illuminating. Now they are treasured memories.

Create Community. The practice of sharing and helping each other – within the family and outside it - was a central part of my experience growing up. I grew up watching my father work with others to build the auditorium annex to the Buddhist temple in Wapato, or play on the baseball team at camp, or bring potatoes and carrots to my elementary school. I saw my mother fixing food during the Depression for so-called "hobos" as they passed through town. I noticed the way she kept a watchful eye on those around her who needed extra help or comfort.

Although I began life in a tightly woven Japanese immigrant community, my world has expanded exponentially over the years to include all kinds of people from all kinds of backgrounds. Today the forces at work in our country are calling on us to be even more intentional about creating communities that are diverse, inclusive and doing good in the world. We must work together in increasingly intersectional ways, as the Japanese American Citizen League does today when they actively support people engaged in the Black Lives Matter movement, assist Sikh communities that have been targeted with violence, or stand with Muslim Americans against hate and Islamophobia.

Slow Down. The world is speeding up for all of us. I recognize now how stress and negativity can affect our relationships, work, and health. We live in an amazing, if also disturbing, time. There is a bounty of media available to us –some useful, others merely a distraction or fake. I hope my children and grandchildren will learn from some of my struggles, and make a point of slowing down, clearing away the clutter, getting out and doing things they enjoy with the people they love and care about. As they know all too well, I have often raced through life without paying close enough attention to the people right in front of me or completing one project before I jumped into another.

Stay Grounded Spiritually. Wise teachers, great books, meaningful experiences and kind friends inspire us to lead fulfilling lives. What can provide even deeper meaning – as I learned from my parents – is to ground ourselves spiritually. I once went to *Esumi-mura* to see the temple my father had gone to as a child and young man. After meeting the priest there, I realized quickly that the Buddhist teachings that were at the root of Papa's life did not come from any building but from putting them in practice. Papa said his prayers and meditated before the *butsudan* every day, sometimes lighting incense or placing citrus fruits or mochi on the altar. Then he went outside to tend his farm and take care of his family.

The same was true for my mother. She did not use any fancy words or proselytize. Yet her teachings and actions clearly came from a deep spiritual center. Being a part of a religious community was important to my parents. But it was how they put Buddha's teachings into practice in their everyday lives and struggles that really mattered.

<u>Persevere</u>. Even with the best of plans, we all hit bumps, detours, and even stop signs on the paths we take. Finding ways to go on takes persistence. One of my favorite stories about Winston Churchill is the story of when he was invited to give a commencement address at Harrow, the public school he attended as a boy. The headmaster, who admonished the graduating students to listen very carefully to the Prime Minister's words of wisdom, introduced him with great aplomb. Then Churchill rose and gave the following address: *"Never give up,"* and sat down.

The headmaster was dumbstruck but quickly commented: "That was very profound advice, Sir. But surely you can add a word or two for our graduates who are so eager to hear more from you." Churchill looked over the student body, walked slowly to the podium and expanded on his speech, bellowing out: *"NEVER, NEVER, GIVE UP,"* and sat down.

My mother arrived at her own understanding and practice of Churchill's maxim, through the wisdom she had gained from Buddhism and her community: stay calm, persevere, don't give up.

I saw her do this all her life, even in her last moments. She was in the hospital by then, in a great deal of pain after surgery. The doctors said that she had less than 24 hours to live. Yet three days later, Mama was still hanging on. I asked my youngest sister Tomiko, a nurse, what was keeping her going. She replied, "Mama's waiting for Shigeko and the others." My sister Shigeko was flying in from Florida, my sister Motoko from New York, my niece Erika from Maryland, and my sister Toyo from Japan.

Mama waited until she saw everyone. Even though she was hurting, she did not complain. She expressed gratitude. She had regained consciousness and her speech for a short time when Toyo arrived. Mama told her, *"Yo o kite kureta, arigato",* or "you did well to come, thank you so much." She would live for three more weeks. Until the end, Mama continued to show the tremendous inner strength and sense of appreciation that characterized her life and inspired all of ours.

Practice Gratitude. It is one thing to be grateful when life is good. To be grateful when things are hard – as my mother did – is a far more difficult feat. But ultimately this is what life asks of us: to find the good in our lives, in others, even in the midst of our struggles. Japanese Buddhists call this "*nembutsu*" – the art of living with appreciation. Rev. Bob Oshita from the Sacramento Buddhist Church describes *nembutsu* in a way that makes good sense to me: "to wake up glad to be alive and go to bed grateful for the day." In my 83rd year of life this is still my practice and good fortune. I hope it will be so for my children and grandchildren and all who come after me.

Kansha

The Japanese word *"kansha"* means to appreciate and thank. I am thankful for all the people – named and unnamed in this memoir – for their presence in my life. I am especially grateful to my family, friends, students, and colleagues for their belief that I had an important life-story to tell.

I want to give special thanks to my daughter, Esumi Fujimoto, for her encouragement and design of the cover of this book. The photo on the front depicts my family at the Driscoll Camp in 1947. I also want to express my appreciation to my wife, Christine Fry, for her support and editorial assistance.

Most of the stories found in this memoir were written over a four-year period in Marcella Lorfing's wonderful memoir writing group in Davis, California. Offered through OLLI (Osher Lifelong Learning Institute), Marcella and my classmates listened to my stories and challenged me to tell more.

Finally, I would like to thank Gerald Ward, a Sacramento City Librarian who helped me bring my stories together into an actual book through the Library's community-based I Street Press.

If anyone reading this book would like to contact me, please email me at ifujimoto@ucdavis.edu. I would enjoy hearing from you.

www.ingramcontent.com/pod-product-compliance
Lightning Source LLC
Chambersburg PA
CBHW071409280526
45787CB00001B/501